Your
30-DAY
JOURNEY
— T·O —
Freedom
From
Shame

YOUR 30-DAY JOURNEY — T·O —

Freedom From Shame

C. W. Neal

THOMAS NELSON PUBLISHERS
Nashville

Published in Nashville, Tennessee, by Oliver-Nelson Books, a division of Thomas Nelson, Inc., Publishers, and distributed in Canada by Lawson Falle, Ltd., Cambridge, Ontario.

The Bible version used in this publication is THE NEW KING JAMES VERSION. Copyright © 1979, 1980, 1982, Thomas Nelson, Inc., Publishers.

Scripture quotation noted NRSV is from the New Revised Standard Version of the Bible. Copyright © 1989 by the Division of Christian Education of the National Council of the Churches of Christ in the United States of America.

The individuals described in this book are composites of real persons whose identities are disguised to protect their privacy.

Printed in the United States of America.

Library of Congress Cataloging-in-Publication Data

Neal, C. W. (Connie W.), 1958–
    Your 30-day journey to freedom from shame. / C.W. Neal.
        p.   cm.
    ISBN 0-8407-9628-5 (pbk.)
    1. Shame.   2. Self-realization.   3. Shame—Religious aspects—Christianity.   4. Self-realization—Religious aspects—Christianity.   I. Title.   II. Title: Your thirty day journey to freedom from shame.
BF575.S45N43   1992
152.4—dc20   92-19061
                                                          CIP

1 2 3 4 5 6 — 97 96 95 94 93 92

Contents

Introduction

Shame is an emotional terrorist. Shame has the power to hold you hostage: to keep you from going where you long to go, from doing what you need to do to be happy and well, from reaching out for relationships with others, which you desperately need. When you are in bondage to shame, you cannot ask for help for fear that others will recognize the awful secret about you, that you aren't as good as they are in some way, that you are deeply flawed. Shame keeps you in bondage by means of blackmail, convincing you that if others ever find out the "truth" about you, you will be utterly rejected, and your life will be ruined.

Shame keeps some people in bondage in shacks with dirt floors. Others are held hostage by shame in castles; they hide behind their image, their wealth, their position, their title, and their work for fear that someone will discover the real them . . . and reject them. Either way, shame is a merciless captor.

When you are imprisoned by shame, you are kept from meeting your legitimate needs in healthy ways. This emotional starvation can be a powerful influence that drives you to adopt unhealthy ways of meeting your needs without ever being truly satisfied.

In this 30-day journey the goal is not to eliminate all shame from your life. The goal is to identify one area where you are shame bound and
follow a process that allows you to break free. The
freedom from shame will release you to go where
you long to go, do what you dream of doing, be
who you truly are.

Your 30-Day Journey to Freedom from Shame
helps you identify areas where you feel imprisoned
by shame and enables you to follow a 30-day program to break free. You will learn step-by-step how
to

- clearly identify healthy and toxic shame in your
  life.
- find the courage to meet emotional needs in
  healthy ways.
- reach out to mentors and friends for healing and
  support.
- experience the freedom to come out of hiding.

The process involves these elements:

- Identifying a specific area of your life where you
  are held hostage by shame and its damaging effects
- Reexamining what caused you to become shame
  bound
- Developing a new understanding of shame-
  binding events in your life that may help you
  realize your identity does not have to be defined
  by those experiences

- Daring to be human (not subhuman or superhuman) and exercising the courage to change
- Doing "honest pretending": taking steps of faith to live out the truth that you are a respectable human being
- Challenging the assumptions that convince you that you are irreparably flawed
- Sorting out hostage-taking shame from legitimate guilt and health-preserving shame; then dealing with each in appropriate ways
- Adopting new rituals and new symbols that acknowledge a new sense of identity
- Developing a maintenance plan to remain free from the bondage of shame in that area of your life

You can think of this book as a menu. It describes many ideas and action steps you can take to nourish yourself in ways that will bring freedom from shame. Reading it without participating in the journey will do no more to free you from shame than reading a menu without ordering and eating the meal will nourish your body or satisfy your hunger. I sincerely hope that you will dare to participate fully in this journey and find the freedom to go where you want to go in life, solve the problems you need to solve, do what you want to do, have more satisfying relationships, and lovingly accept your value as the person you truly are.

1

Your Commitment to Your Journey

Your journey to freedom from shame requires a firm commitment. If your life is in bondage to shame, your deepest beliefs tell you that you are flawed; something is inherently wrong with you that separates you from other people who are normal, acceptable, and lovable. Living in a state of chronic shame is painful. You have been willing to try to manage the pain rather than confront it because shame is also powerfully intimidating. You fear that if you ever dare to take a close look at the shame keeping you in bondage, you may confirm your worst fears about yourself. Therefore, you have accepted the pain and limitations imposed by shame as a way of avoiding the possibility of being exposed for who you believe yourself to be.

This journey marks the beginning of a confrontation with your captor—unhealthy shame that has blackmailed you into a life far less satisfying than you desire. This journey will lead you in the direction of your deepest fears, and along the way, you may uncover areas of pain that have yet to be dealt with. To take this journey, you will need a glimmer of hope, a tiny speck of faith, and a fair amount of courage. You will put all of them into action through your determined commitment to complete this journey.

You have demonstrated a glimmer of hope by picking up this book. Your hopes for happiness, a better life, healthy family relationships, a degree of intimacy that will allow you to give and receive true love, a reasonable measure of success, satisfying friendships, and peace with yourself draw you to venture on this journey.

Faith is being willing to do something to reach toward what you hope for in the future. You exercise faith every day. When you reach for the light switch, you are doing something you believe will give you light. When you board an airplane, you are taking a step of faith in hopes of reaching your destination. Your willingness to try to follow this 30-day journey shows that you have the faith needed. Your hope says, "I hope I am not as irreparably damaged as I believe myself to be." Your faith steps out in the direction of a journey to find freedom from shame and the life waiting beyond the bondage.

Courage is not an absence of fear. Courage is determining to use your strength and resources to take steps in the right direction, even though you are afraid. You can find courage within yourself. You can draw courage from your trust in a loving God who will never leave you in the midst of the battles of life. You can draw courage from others who have conquered their shame to discover a wealth of life beyond the bondage. You can draw courage from people who love you and believe the best of you. Gather up all the courage within your reach and determine to make a firm commitment to this journey.

PERSONAL EVALUATION

· What hopes cause you to desire freedom from shame?
· Do you have a tiny measure of faith that says, "Maybe there is hope for freedom from shame; I am willing to try"?
· What will be the source of your courage to keep you moving in the face of your fears?
· Are you willing to make this commitment to yourself?
· If you are not willing or are hesitant, ask yourself what feelings accompany your unwillingness. Anger? Defensiveness? Fear? Sadness? Can you talk with someone about these feelings?

ACTION: *YOUR PERSONAL COMMITMENT*

I, _____, am serious about my desire to gain freedom from shame so that I can go where I long to go, do what I want to do, and be who I truly am with a sense of dignity and self-respect.

For the next 30 days I will invest the time to read each day's passage and reserve thirty minutes of quiet time to reflect on the issues addressed. I plan to take this time each *(circle one)* morning, lunchtime, afternoon, evening, or before bedtime. I will honestly consider the personal evaluations, take the action steps (to the best of my ability), and keep a journal of feelings as they emerge. I will share this journey with someone I trust; I will make myself accountable to this person to complete the journey, and I will look to this person for encouragement.

I understand that to reach this goal, I must be willing to exercise the courage to look at myself carefully and to endeavor to meet all challenges with perseverance.

I am willing to move toward truth, even if it is upsetting, and to look back to gain a new perspective from which I can move forward to a better life. I am willing to reexamine my beliefs about myself, my way of life, and my relationships to make changes that can free me from shame.

I make this commitment to myself this _____ day of _____, 19____.

_____
Signature

REFLECTION

This section will suggest topics to consider during your daily quiet time. You may be tempted to skip this part of your journey because reflecting on issues related to shame is often painful. Facing the pain—and moving past it to deal with the issues causing the pain—is the only way to eliminate it. It is something like removing a splinter. Your first reaction is to avoid touching the area around a splinter because it will hurt. However, if you don't get to the splinter and remove it, you will live with ongoing pain as the sore festers. Your shame may be the festering symptom of a specific problem that needs to be confronted. During your times of reflection, try to see the pain as a helpful indicator of where you need to give your life attention and care.

You may want to be alone and undisturbed for your times of reflection, or you may opt to reflect on these issues with your journey companion. When feelings arise, try to accept them and allow yourself to feel them. You may want to write out the feelings or memories that occur. If you begin to feel overwhelmed, contact someone who can help you come to grips with your overwhelming emotions.

ENCOURAGEMENT

Many people have found their way free from the bondage imposed by shame, and you can, too. A life is waiting for you that you might never have imagined because you disqualified yourself as someone unworthy of the good things in life. Don't give up on yourself! You can learn to see yourself differently.

FOOD FOR THOUGHT

What you commit yourself to become determines what you are.

—Dr. Tony Campolo

Finding a Companion for Your Journey

The path of shame is a lonely one, trodden in self-imposed isolation. You may be surrounded by others, but they are not allowed into the inner chambers of your life. You fear that they will discover the real you, and you believe that knowing you, as you perceive yourself to be, will hurt them and you.

You may isolate yourself in an attempt to protect the ones you care about from the pain of being exposed to you. The lepers of old separated themselves from society, living in colonies with others who were diseased in the same way. They would announce their presence by calling out the warning, "Unclean! Unclean!" in an effort to protect anyone they might encounter from contracting the dread disease. You may separate yourself from the people you care about most. You may do things to purposely drive them away because you believe their involvement with you would be to their ultimate ruin. In your own way of seeing yourself, you are demonstrating loving care for others whenever you spare them the pain you believe inherent in a relationship with someone flawed, as you believe yourself to be.

You may also keep people you care about most at a distance for your self-protection. You believe that if others knew the real you, they would reject you or despise you. Therefore, you may be afraid to risk the rejection of those whose love you most desire. You may act out your anger at being rejected by becoming hostile toward others or behaving in socially unacceptable ways as a dare to see if anyone will see beyond the bluster to find something lovable in you that you are not convinced of yourself. You may keep them at a distance by resorting to offensive behavior, by brandishing the shield of your anger or rage, by attacking them or rejecting them first before they have the chance to reject you, or by running away and making yourself unavailable.

You may keep those you care about most at a distance from the real you by pretending to be whoever you think they want you to be. You start out hoping that they will accept the mask you wear and love you for it, but even if they do love you on those terms, you cannot receive the love. You are left isolated, hiding within the walls of the image you present. You may give beyond the call of duty without ever giving them access to the real you hidden within. You may end up angry and resentful because you have to keep up the act to receive their love, or you may go through the motions of having a love relationship without ever being known. You have still isolated yourself, although they may never know it.

Whether you are motivated by wanting to protect them or yourself or both, whether you drive them away or live in a counterfeit relationship, the result is self-isolation. You may settle for transient or shallow relationships or try to live as best you can without developing relationships at all. Your reasoning may be that whenever anyone gets close to you, someone gets hurt, so you are trying to make it through life with as little pain as possible. Although this response to shame is understandable, it is not fulfilling. Gaining freedom from shame involves beginning to walk away from a life-style of isolation and toward building satisfying relationships.

Finding a companion for your journey is a step in this direction. Your companion doesn't need to be someone you feel safe to open yourself up to completely because that is not the role the person will play in your journey. The person should be someone you can feel reasonably safe to turn to for encouragement and to whom you can confide that you are dealing with issues of shame.

Picture a long-distance runner who has support personnel driving alongside in a car. The runner goes through the paces but has arranged for a support team to be available whenever needed. In this journey you will have moments when an encouraging voice, a proud smile, and a nod of approval will prove extremely valuable. You are looking for a companion

- who will encourage you.
- with a positive outlook on life.
- who does not see you as all saint or all sinner.

- who does not have a personal interest in trying to change you.
- you are not trying to impress.
- who will allow you to express honest thoughts and sincere feelings without trying to fix them or negate them.
- who will give you honest feedback.
- who will keep your confidences.
- who is committed to continue to love you.

PERSONAL EVALUATION

Take a moment to think of someone who could act as your companion on this journey. Identify the person you would most like to support you along the way. Also decide on a second choice if that person is unavailable.

You may think of friends, people in a support group, relatives (*only* if they are supportive and can keep your journey confidential), members of your church, synagogue, or other organizations.

ACTION

Contact the person you have in mind to be your companion for the journey, and ask the person to do so.

REFLECTION

- How do you feel about sharing this experience with someone else?
- Are you fortunate to have a circle of support per-

sons so that finding someone was relatively easy?
- If you couldn't find someone today, are you willing to keep trying?
- Can you look to God for additional support as you continue on your journey?

ENCOURAGEMENT

Just reaching out for support and telling someone that you are beginning a journey like this take courage. You deserve to give yourself credit for your effort. If you didn't find anyone or were reluctant to ask, that's understandable. But you need to have someone to turn to along the way.

FOOD FOR THOUGHT

Two are better than one, because they have a good reward for their toil. For if they fall, one will lift up the other; but woe to one who is alone and falls and does not have another to help.
                                    —Ecclesiastes 4:9–10 NRSV

Understanding Healthy and Unhealthy Shame

Shame is the inner pain that comes from accepting the belief that something inherently wrong with you makes you less than others. It is quite different from feeling guilty for some wrong you have committed. Shame is feeling guilty for the kind of person you believe yourself to be, feeling guilty for your very existence.

In his book *Healing the Shame that Binds You*, John Bradshaw says shame

> is a healthy human power which can become a true sickness of the soul. There are two forms of shame: nourishing shame and toxic/life destroying shame. As toxic shame, it is an excruciatingly internal experience of unexpected exposure. It is a cut felt primarily from the inside. It divides us from ourselves and from others.

Think of healthy shame as your personal, moral, and emotional smoke detector. Just as a smoke detector can forewarn you of the danger of fire that could destroy your home if left to burn unabated, healthy shame signals whenever you are about to enter a potentially dangerous personal situation. As long as you heed the warning given by healthy shame, avoiding behavior and situations that are shameful, you will benefit from your internal security system.

PERSONAL EVALUATION

Here is a comparison between healthy and unhealthy shame. Rate yourself on a scale of one to ten for each item (one means that this is not descriptive of you at any time; ten means that this is descriptive of you most of the time).

With Healthy Shame . . .   *Rating*

You see your behavior as separate from your identity. You may do something bad, but you don't take that as evidence you are essentially a bad person. . . . . . .   _____

You see your experience as separate from your identity. Something bad may happen to you or you may be treated abusively, but you don't assume that you deserve such treatment. . . . .   _____

You see normal lapses, errors, and failures as part of being human. They may act as catalysts, prompting you to make changes toward a more positive direction in life, but they do not overwhelm you. .   _____

You see avoidance of shame-producing behavior as a way to protect yourself from pain and destruction. . . . .   _____

You see violation of your boundaries as a problem that needs to be corrected to reduce the discomfort of the shame you experience. ———

You trust that shame is a temporary feeling of discomfort, which will dissipate when you move away from the violation of your boundaries. . . . . ———

You see your life as valuable and shame as something built into your being to protect the sanctity of your life. . . . . ———

You try to live within the boundaries of socially acceptable behavior and take steps to fit in with society. You act in ways that protect your privacy and practice discretion in your relationships. . . . ———

Add your ratings for these eight items. If your total equals

39 or under You need help (professional help, further reading on the subject) in developing healthy shame.

40 or over You're generally healthy, but you may need to work on specific areas where you have difficulty.

With Unhealthy Shame . . .   *Rating*

You see wrong behavior or failings as a reflection of your true identity. When you do something bad or make a mistake, you see that as evidence you are flawed. . . . . ———

You accept part of the blame when you are violated by others. You see yourself as someone who deserves to be abused or treated poorly.   _____

You see normal lapses, errors, and failures as the revelation of your true nature, which is flawed, rather than as a part of being human. You may feel overwhelmed when you experience such a lapse because you think it reveals that something is terribly wrong with you. . . . .   _____

You see avoidance of the shame-producing behavior or life-style as futile, since you believe the behavior or lifestyle is the natural result of being the kind of person you see yourself to be. . . .   _____

You consider trying to change your life for the better as living a lie or being hypocritical. You believe your steps in a positive direction are phony, and you negate them instead of viewing them as evidence that you can change. . . . .   _____

Whenever you experience a normal human failing, make an honest mistake, suffer a disappointment, violate your moral standards, or have your boundaries violated by others, it may trigger a downward spiral of depression or addictive behavior. . . . .   _____

You may appear to others to be utterly shameless in some or all areas of your life. When you shut down the influence of healthy shame, you lose the strength of your boundaries. You may eventually be worn down to the point that you give in to your overwhelming shame and act out in ways that show no sense of healthy shame and no awareness of legitimate moral guilt. . . . .   ———

Add your ratings for these seven items. If your total equals

35 or over   You are dealing with a significant degree of unhealthy shame.

34 or under   You are probably generally healthy. Everyone experiences shame to some degree, and so if your score is 34 or under, your shame is probably manageable.

ACTION

Write out a description of how healthy shame operates in your life at this time. Also note any specific experiences that might have violated your healthy shame throughout your life, causing a breakdown of your barriers or a shutoff of the influence of healthy shame.

Write out a description of how unhealthy shame operates in your life at this time. Note specific areas where you feel inferior to others because of a sense of shame that makes you fear something is wrong with you.

REFLECTION

Looking at the contrast between healthy and unhealthy shame may spark feelings of being less than normal if you score high on unhealthy shame and low on healthy shame. If you see a high degree of unhealthy shame influencing your life, focus on the truth that your identity is held captive by shame. Your true identity is *not* defined by your shame. Try to separate your realization of the degree to which shame affects you from your definition of your identity.

ENCOURAGEMENT

To whatever degree your healthy sense of shame has been damaged, it can be restored. To whatever degree your life has been damaged by unhealthy shame, you can find healing for the brokenness. In whatever areas you are held captive by shame, you can break free to venture into a new way of life.

FOOD FOR THOUGHT

And they were both naked, the man and his wife, and were not ashamed.

—Genesis 2:25

Identifying the Symptoms of Your Shame

Unhealthy shame is an internal matter. People may look at you and never dream your life is limited by shame. You may appear to others to be far different from the way you see yourself, since shame causes you to cover up the real you. There are specific symptoms of unhealthy shame. Consider which of the following symptoms are evident in your life. You may also identify other symptoms not included here that are specific to you. Take note of them as you go through the list.

PERSONAL EVALUATION

Place a check next to any of these symptoms you believe may be evidence of shame in your life.

☐ 1. You simply can't bring yourself to do things, go places, or be around people because you feel intimidated.

☐ 2. You experience recurrent bouts of depression.

☐ 3. You are in self-isolation: physically or emotionally distancing yourself from others, particularly those you most care about.

☐ 4. You pretend to be other than you are.

☐ 5. You use addictive-compulsive behavior to medicate inner pain and self-loathing.

☐ 6. You exaggerate and/or lie about yourself, your accomplishments, and your life-style; you brag and name-drop.

☐ 7. Your public identity and your private self are markedly different.

☐ 8. You exhibit suicidal tendencies.

Shame is terribly painful as a chronic state of self-loathing or as a crisis when there is the threat that the private self may be exposed or humiliated publicly.

Shame causes you to struggle continually with the thought that maybe the world would be better off without you.

Sudden exposure of any shameful aspect of life may prompt a suicide attempt. One teenage girl who had been molested throughout childhood attempted suicide when another person was publicly exposed for sexual immorality at the church she attended. She happened to know that he, too, had been molested as a child. In the hospital after the attempt she explained, "When I saw what they do to people like me, how they want to get rid of us, I figured I would spare them the trouble of finding out my secrets and destroying me the way they destroyed him. I figured I should just go ahead and do God the favor of getting rid of myself."

☐ 9. You assume the blame when someone treats you poorly or hurts you.

Some victims of rape or sexual abuse feel

that they must have done something to invite the attack or to encourage continued abuse.

☐10. You make excuses for people who abuse you or treat you with disrespect.

☐11. You are unable to accept yourself as only human; instead, you see yourself as subhuman or superhuman.

You are unable to accept both the good and the bad within you; rather, you cling to a view of yourself that is all bad or all good, or you alternate between the two.

☐12. You keep secrets you feel bound to carry with you to the grave.

☐13. You keep a shameful part of your life separate from the rest of your life, even in your own mind, so that your behavior in one area is markedly different from the rest of your life.

This separate part may violate your values and eventually threaten your well-being.

☐14. You deny the nature and severity of your addictions.

☐15. You lose yourself in the needs of others, busying yourself taking care of others, rescuing, trying to control, fix, or change them, and trying to solve their problems while neglecting your life.

☐16. You feel driven to achieve, overachieve, and excel to feel OK about yourself; you try to prove your worth by what you do.

☐17. You focus on the flaws and failings of others;

being judgmental and critical draws attention away from you or consoles you that you are not as bad as the object of your criticism.

☐18. You defy societal norms: dressing, acting, and relating in ways that are socially unacceptable. If you defy the rules of society, you can console yourself that any rejection is the rejection of your appearance or manners, and you can distance yourself from taking the rejection personally.

☐19. You associate primarily with people on an extreme end of the social ladder.

Some people associate with those they view as losers because that is the only group they feel they belong with and can be accepted by. Others associate only with people of status because they derive their sense of self-worth from being accepted by those they believe to be above them.

☐20. You break off relationships with those you care about deeply before they have a chance to know the real you and reject you.

☐21. You fear expressing your honest opinions and feelings; you adapt your opinions to try to match those expressed by whoever you are associating with at the time.

☐22. You are lonely.

☐23. You fear being found out as a phony.

☐24. You are a perfectionist: trying to make up for who you are by doing everything perfectly.

☐25. You fear failure, which keeps you from trying new ventures.

☐26. You are unable to ask for help because you feel that admitting your need exposes your area of inadequacy.

One young mother was having a hard time coping with the demands of caring for her infant son. She refused to ask for help because she felt deeply inadequate as a mother. To her, admitting that she didn't know how to perform mothering tasks was an admission that she was a failure as a woman and a person. Another example is the person who cleans the house before the maid arrives because he or she doesn't want to be thought of negatively.

☐27. You resist setting personal goals in the areas where you have a sense of shame.

Action

Review the items you checked as symptoms of shame in your life. Choose the three that are most prevalent. Describe specific incidents where these three symptoms of shame were manifested recently.

Reflection

Consider the effects of these symptoms of shame on your life and relationships. How do you feel when you realize the effects shame is having on your life?

Considering the Shame-Depression Connection

Shame and depression are closely related. If you are suffering from depression, you will have many of the same feelings and symptoms as someone suffering from shame. Living with shame and being unable to break free from its bondage can lead to recurrent bouts of depression. It may be hard to tell which came first, the depression or the shame. Since some depression is a physiological condition experienced emotionally, you need to determine if you are dealing with clinical depression, which needs to be treated medically, or with issues of shame that bring on feelings of depression. If you are suffering from depression that has a physical cause, you need to handle the physical problem first and then the emotional issues. Otherwise you will waste your time and effort wrestling with emotional-relational-psychological issues that may disappear when the physical problem is treated medically.

Depression can be caused by a chemical imbalance in the brain. In the human brain, neurotransmitters are chemicals that carry messages from one nerve ending across a tiny gap to the next nerve ending and then return to prepare to carry the next. If a deficiency in your body chemistry occurred in your arms or legs, you would experience limitations in the use of those parts of your body. When there is a deficiency of neurotransmitters in your brain, the result is depression.

Having a chemical deficiency in the brain can inhibit your ability to function, think, and feel normally. Shame is deeply rooted in the belief that you are somehow flawed. If you are suffering from a chemical imbalance in the brain, you will not feel normal because you are not—in the sense that your brain is not able to function as it should until your brain chemistry is brought back into balance.

You can have hope and help. In recent years medical science has discovered various antidepressant medications that restore the brain chemistry to balance, replenishing the deficiency in the neurotransmitters and restoring brain function to normal. Although that is not the case for everyone, you should consider the possibility and eliminate it before you move on.

PERSONAL EVALUATION

Here are some symptoms of clinical depression. Consider whether you may be dealing primarily with depression that has feelings of shame as one presenting symptom. Check off any of these symptoms prevalent in your life. Take special note if your symptoms of depression are often unrelated to specific events that would understandably cause someone to feel depressed.

Symptoms of Depression

- Feeling down, sad, depressed
- Loss of interest in pleasurable activities and relationships
- Moodiness that lasts for prolonged periods of time, unrelated to whether the circumstances of life are good or bad
- Emotions out of control, crying easily, having outbursts of anger
- Lack of motivation to do anything
- Sleep disturbances: trouble sleeping or sleeping excessively
- Appetite disturbances: loss of appetite; insatiable cravings; eating disorders
- Reduction or loss of sex drive
- Constant fatigue; decreased energy level not related to overexertion
- General thoughts of death and/or suicide
- Unable to concentrate; thought processes slow and disjointed
- Simple decision making an overwhelming task
- A negative outlook on life even when the circumstances are positive
- Intense feelings of guilt and shame
- Feelings of worthlessness; feeling unwanted, unloved, dirty, or sinful
- Unable to function well socially
- Unable or unmotivated to care for personal needs
- Overreacting to everyday difficulties and disappointments

• Chronic physical pain, headaches, or anxiety attacks

ACTION

Make an appointment to get a complete physical examination in conjunction with a psychological evaluation. Contact a recovery treatment hospital, or ask your family doctor for a referral. Make the commitment and begin a program of exercising, eating a healthful diet, and getting adequate rest to eliminate physical problems that may underlie or contribute to your experience of shame.

REFLECTION

• If you had to guess, would you say that your feelings of shame emanate from depression or that your feelings of depression emanate from shame?
• Did you make an appointment for physical and psychological evaluations? If not, what were your reasons?

ENCOURAGEMENT

When you get thorough medical and psychological examinations and begin to care for your physical health, you can dramatically improve your ability to move toward freedom from shame.

Breaking the Shame-Addiction Cycle

You cannot gain freedom from shame while you are actively medicating the pain of life by relying on addictive-compulsive behavior. Shame and addictions feed on one another. You must deal with your issues of shame and addictive-compulsive behavior simultaneously.

The addictive process involves using a mood-altering substance or experience to temporarily escape the pain of life. When you give in to your addiction, you feel better for a while. But once the emotional high dissipates, you need progressively more of whatever you use to get the previous level of relief. Eventually, you violate previously held boundaries. What was once considered taboo or off limits becomes something you allow, even though you offend your conscience. You then have to deal with guilt, self-condemnation, and the consequences of your behavior while under the influence of your addiction. When you once again face yourself and the consequences of your behavior, there is more fuel for the fire of shame already burning within you. Your aggravated feelings of shame cause tremendous pain. You are drawn back to the addictive substance or experience in hopes of deadening the pain that feels overwhelming.

The cycle looks something like this:

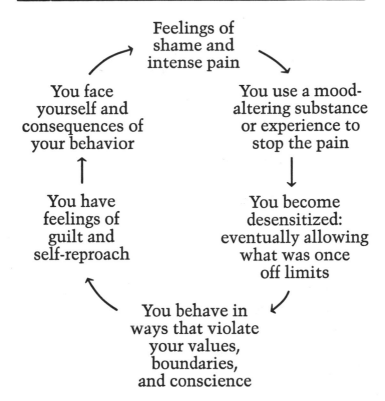

Feelings of
shame and
intense pain

You face
yourself and
consequences of
your behavior

You use a mood-
altering substance
or experience to
stop the pain

You have
feelings of
guilt and
self-reproach

You become
desensitized:
eventually allowing
what was once
off limits

You behave in
ways that violate
your values,
boundaries,
and conscience

Shame will drag you back into addictive-compulsive behavior, and addictive-compulsive behavior will drag you back into shame. It is a vicious cycle that must be stopped at the point of the addiction while also dealing with the underlying issues of shame.

PERSONAL EVALUATION

· What do you do to temporarily alter your mood when you are feeling pain associated with unhealthy shame?
· What substances or experiences do you use to escape the pain of living your life?

Place a check next to any addictions you have used at any time. Circle any of these addictive-compulsive behaviors you currently use (within the last six months).

Alcohol
Codependency
Compulsive gambling
Compulsive overeating
Compulsive spending
Narcotics
Relational/romance addiction
Religious addiction
Sex addiction (including the use of pornography or any form of sexual stimulation)
Workaholism
Other:_____

ACTION

Do something today to seek treatment for your addictive or compulsive behavior. Call a treatment program; attend a support group or a twelve-step group; tell someone that you realize you may have an addiction to deal with; make an appointment with a counselor who specializes in helping persons with your particular addiction.

REFLECTION

How do you see addiction and shame interrelating in your life?

ENCOURAGEMENT

Living without your addiction does not have to mean ongoing pain for you. By dealing with shame-related issues at the same time you seek treatment for addiction, you have the best chance possible of finding a way to happiness. You can find a way to live without the desperate need to medicate yourself to enjoy life.

FOOD FOR THOUGHT

You will not die from sobriety.

—Anonymous

Defining Your Goals for Shame Reduction

Goal setting poses a formidable challenge to someone in bondage to shame. Shame tells you there is no use trying to reach a goal because you will only fail. Shame warns that having a clearly defined goal will clearly prove your deficiency. If you deeply believe or fear there is something inherently wrong with you, you will resist setting specific goals that could be used to measure your failure. In your mind, failure to reach a goal is translated to mean you are a failure as a person.

One indicator that shame has you bound in a particular area of life is that you give up on having goals in that area since the risk of failure is too great. In areas where shame is not a factor, you feel more comfortable setting goals since you believe you have a chance to reach them. If you don't reach them, you don't interpret that to mean something is deeply wrong with you. As you learn to set and reach goals that reduce your level of unhealthy shame, you will find more courage and freedom to set goals in other areas as well.

PERSONAL EVALUATION

By considering your personal goals in various areas of life, you will be better able to identify areas where shame is limiting you the most. The areas where you have no goals and no desire to set any are the areas most inhibited by shame. For our purposes here, you can define a *goal* as (1) a clearly defined statement of your desires and dreams (2) set in measurable terms and (3) pursued within a specific time frame.

In each of the following areas of life (family, career, spiritual, financial, home, physical, mental/ intellectual, social) ask yourself three questions:

1. Do I know what I desire and dream of in this area?
2. Have I clarified my desires and dreams into specific measurable terms so I can know when I have reached my goals?
3. Am I pursuing my goals within a specified time frame?

ACTION

Reducing shame is a legitimate goal in and of itself. However, since shame is primarily an obstacle to setting and reaching other goals, you will focus your attention on reducing shame enough to move beyond some of the limitations shame has imposed in the area of life you have selected. Complete the following sentences:

Shame keeps me from doing . . .
Shame causes me to feel uncomfortable whenever I . . .
Shame keeps me from going . . .

Shame keeps me from trying . . .
Shame keeps me from having a relationship with . . .
Shame keeps me from being . . .

Now complete these sentences:

I want to overcome shame in this area of my life so I can experience the freedom
   to do this . . .
   to feel more comfortable whenever I . . .
   to try this . . .
   to develop a relationship with . . .
   to become . . .

From what you have written in the exercise, select one short-term goal to reach by the end of your 30-day journey. Specifically describe your goal so that you will know when you have reached it. Make this goal small enough to reach and yet beyond what you are able to do right now.

Select a more challenging goal in this same area that you want to reach within the next year. Again clearly describe the accomplishment of the goal so that you can tell when you have reached it.

Select another goal in this area that represents what you would like to be able to do if shame were not a factor. Make it a long-term goal that you would like to reach within the next ten years.

REFLECTION

- What did you learn about yourself by considering the goals you have and do not have?
- In which areas are you *not* inhibited by shame?
- How do you feel about yourself in these areas that differs from how you feel about yourself in areas where you are in bondage to shame? Consider the possibility that someday you may be as free in all areas of life as you are in the areas where you currently experience freedom from shame.

ENCOURAGEMENT

You can set and reach your goals. You are already practicing and reaching your daily goal of taking the steps and reflecting on this 30-day journey. Once you learn to achieve your goal of gaining freedom from shame in one small area of life, you will be able to continue setting goals and achieving them to reduce shame in other areas. Once healthy shame is restored, you will discover the joy and power of setting and reaching goals in every important area of life.

FOOD FOR THOUGHT

A goal properly set is partially reached.
—Zig Ziglar

Envisioning Benefits of Freedom from Shame

The story of Cinderella is a story of gaining freedom from shame. Cinderella couldn't go to the ball because she wasn't like the other girls in the kingdom. The invitation said that all eligible maidens were to attend. But Cinderella's stepmother and wicked stepsisters made it clear to her that she did not qualify. Cinderella was told that girls like her were not eligible for the good things of life. They pointed out all the evidence: she was just a scullery maid; she was dirty; she didn't have the proper dress; she didn't have refined manners; she had to work and couldn't enjoy the luxury of taking time away for parties. Their ridicule and abuse almost convinced Cinderella to give up hope. She almost conceded. Maybe girls like her weren't eligible for the good things of life. In her moment of shame and disappointment Cinderella threw herself to the ground and sobbed, "Now, I'll never go to the ball."

The turning point in the story came when Cinderella's fairy godmother appeared and rekindled the dream within her heart. Thanks to her fairy godmother's belief in her, Cinderella was able to envision herself as one of the eligible maidens instead of an outcast.

The benefits of freedom from shame for Cinderella were much the same as the benefits you will receive when you gain freedom from shame. She was welcome to attend the party. She was able to fit in and feel that she belonged. She was able to acquire the things she needed to go where she wanted to go and do what she wanted to do. She was able to bring out the beauty and grace that were always within her but were covered with the rags of poverty and the ashes in which she lived. She was able to take advantage of the opportunity for new and wonderful relationships. She was able to hold her head high with a sense of self-respect. She was able to have fun, to laugh and dance and sing and, most important, to give and receive love. Ultimately, she was able to escape the abusive home and family life that contributed to keeping her in bondage to shame. She was able to defy the lie that said she was eligible for nothing more than a life locked away in a dirty tower as someone's slave.

A turning point in your story will come the moment you are sincerely able to envision what life could become when you are freed from the bondage of shame. Dare to dream of what life could be like if you knew that you were eligible for the good things, that you were not disqualified.

PERSONAL EVALUATION

- What would be different for you if you knew you were welcome at the party of life and that you were eligible for the life you once dreamed of?

- How would life be different if you were able to fit in and feel that you belong? If you were able to acquire the things you need to go where you want to go and do what you want to do? If you were able to discover what is good within you, what has been covered with your own version of rags and ashes of your shameful life?
- How would life be if you were able to reach out to others and share of yourself so that you could successfully manage opportunities for new and satisfying relationships?
- How would it feel to hold your head high with a sense of self-respect? To have fun, to laugh and dance and sing, without feeling inhibited? To give and receive love?
- What would it mean for you to escape the abusive situations and relationships that contribute to keeping you in bondage to shame?
- How would it feel to be vindicated before the eyes of those who shamed you and told you people like you are not eligible for the good things in life?

ACTION

After considering all the questions, describe what you think your life might become if you were completely freed from the bondage of shame. Write your description in as much detail as possible; describe the changes in your living situation, family life, career, social life, spiritual life, finances, physical well-being, appearance, education, and so on.

Describe how you would feel, what you would do, where you would go, what you would become, and what new adventures you would seek.

ENCOURAGEMENT

You are invited to the party of life. God created you as a valuable human being with infinite worth and tremendous potential. You live in a country where your personal freedoms are protected. Shame is standing between you and the party of life, but you can get beyond it.

FOOD FOR THOUGHT

In the depth of winter I finally learned that there was in me an invincible summer.
—Albert Camus

Clearing Away Legitimate Guilt

Guilt and shame are closely related, often becoming a confused jumble of painful emotions. When guilt and shame become intertwined, the accumulation of pain, the desire to escape yourself, and the weight of your burdens can threaten to overwhelm you. By identifying and resolving legitimate guilt, you get your shame more clearly into focus so that you can begin to deal with it appropriately.

Guilt and shame are similar in that both can cause you to want to hide, distance yourself from God and others, and try to make amends to feel better. Both can evoke deep feelings of sadness, fear, self-loathing, and remorse. The difference between legitimate guilt and shame is that guilt is related to behavior and shame is related to your being. With guilt, you are troubled by what you have done; with shame, you are troubled by who you are.

True guilt is experienced when you do something that is wrong or fail to do what you know to be right when it is in your power to do it. Legitimate guilt also occurs when you break a commitment that you entered into willingly. The solution for legitimate guilt is to accept responsibility for having violated moral boundaries, confess the exact nature of your wrongs to God, yourself, and another human being, and seek forgiveness. You also reduce your burden of guilt when you identify persons who have been harmed by your wrongs and make amends to them, except when to do so would injure them or others. (This is a powerful part of the twelve-step process of recovery.)

Healthy shame may evoke feelings of sadness and disappointment when you realize there are limitations to what you can do and be for others, but these feelings do not overwhelm you. Unhealthy shame causes you to condemn yourself on the basis of who you are and the limitations within your life. With unhealthy shame, you are overwhelmed with sadness and self-hatred whenever you realize that you are less than the person you wish you were and whenever your limitations keep you from being the person you wish you could be.

You may try to rid yourself of guilt by throwing out all the rules, choosing to deny your allegiance to previously held moral standards. Choosing to ignore the rules doesn't eliminate the guilt. It just requires more energy to suppress the feelings of guilt you are left to deal with on your own because shame has cut you off from the One who has the ability to forgive you and cleanse you.

PERSONAL EVALUATION

- Are guilt and shame clearly distinguished in your life?

- Do you believe there is no forgiveness for people like you?
- When confronted with your personal limitations, do you feel a reasonable measure of sadness and disappointment or an overwhelming weight of self-condemnation?
- How has shame cut you off from the forgiveness offered by God?
- How do you deal with your feelings of guilt if you are cut off or distanced from God?

ACTION

After each of the following items, there is a scale that represents a continuum between two poles, guilt and shame. The right side represents shame (who you are and your personal limitations); the left side represents legitimate guilt (related to specific behavior or the lack thereof). Mark a point on the continuum that represents to what degree the item is most often associated with guilt or shame.

For example, if you want to avoid people generally because you feel inadequate and fear their possible rejection of you as a person, place the mark on the shame side of the line.

Example   GUILT   SHAME
Feeling like you are   ├──────────┼──┤
inadequate and that
others will reject you

	GUILT	SHAME
1. Feeling like you want to hide and avoid people	├───────────┤	
2. Feeling like you want to distance yourself from God	├─────────────┤	
3. Feeling like you want to make amends or compensate for failure	├───────────┤	
4. Feelings of sadness	├──────────┤	
5. Feelings of fear	├────────────┤	
6. Feelings of self-loathing	├──────────┤	
7. Feelings of remorse and regret	├──────────┤	

REFLECTION

Here's how to live without wallowing in guilt:

Step One Whenever you experience guilty feelings, stop to examine their source.

Step Two Identify behaviors causing you legitimate guilt. (In a twelve-step program you would do this during Step Four when you take a complete moral inventory.)

Step Three Acknowledge the exact nature of your wrongs to God, yourself, and another human being.

Step Four Accept the forgiveness offered by God.

Step Five If necessary, seek out someone who understands the grace and love of God to help you learn to accept God's forgiveness.

FOOD FOR THOUGHT

If we say that we have no sin, we deceive ourselves, and the truth is not in us. If we confess our sins, He is faithful and just to forgive us our sins and to cleanse us from all unrighteousness.

—1 John 1:8–9

Identifying Sources of Your Shame

Identifying the sources of unhealthy shame is important so you can find resources to deal with the roots of shame and heal any emotional injury. The sources of internalized shame can be classified in three categories: (1) shame assigned to you by others; (2) shame derived from chronic exposure to a shameful environment; and (3) shame resulting from an isolated branding experience.

1. Shame assigned to you by others would involve what you are told or taught about yourself leading you to believe there is something inherently wrong with you. Assigned shame does not always become internalized shame. If you are assigned shame at a time when you are already confident in your identity or the shame is assigned by someone who is not important in your life, you will have an easier time resisting the condemnation as untrue about you. However, if the assigned shame comes at a time when your identity is still being formed in childhood and adolescence, you will be more prone to accept the condemnation as true. When the condemnation comes from someone close to you, someone important in your life, or someone to whom you have revealed yourself, it has greater power to influence your view of yourself.

Here are some specific examples of assigned shame:

- Something you were taught about yourself at an early age
- Verbal abuse, being called names that define your worth in negative terms, such as stupid, idiot, good-for-nothing, ugly, or being told you will never amount to anything, and so on
- Being identified as the scapegoat of the family, the troublemaker, the black sheep, and so on
- Being teased by other children and told that you deserve to be picked on because there is something wrong with you or your family
- Being shamed into submission
- Something that you deduced from what people told you about yourself through nonverbal cues, such as being discriminated against on the basis of race, sex, color, physical handicap, or religious beliefs
- Being punished for your individuality

2. Shame derived from chronic exposure to a shameful environment would involve living in ongoing circumstances that degrade your human dignity, situations that make you feel abnormal or inferior to your peers. Again not all people living in these shameful circumstances internalize the shame. It depends on what other sources of feedback and support you receive to shape your self-image, your developmental stage and awareness level during the seasons when the shameful envi-

ronment exists, the degree to which your life is directly affected by the shameful circumstances, and the duration of the shameful situation.

The following examples illustrate chronic environmentally based shame:

- Parental neglect so that your basic needs are not met
- Socially unacceptable behavior within the family that is known publicly within the community
- Living within a family where there is alcoholism, drug addiction, or compulsions that cause life to be out of control and unpredictable; and where personal boundaries are often violated
- Living with ongoing sexual and/or physical abuse
- Growing up in a "perfect" family where there is constant criticism for any failure to meet the expected standards
- Poverty: living in filthy conditions, wearing clothing that is socially unacceptable, and so on
- Physical abnormalities

3. Shame resulting from an isolated branding experience would involve a particular incident that overshadows the rest of your life and leaves you feeling indelibly marked in a negative way. An isolated experience has the greatest power to produce shame when it touches close to an area where you secretly feel vulnerable or fear you truly are inadequate, and when there is public exposure.

Some examples of shame resulting from an isolated branding experience include the following:

- Violating your moral standards in a way that is shocking to you
- Being publicly exposed in an area where you have done wrong or feel vulnerable
- A forced violation of your sexual boundaries, such as rape or other violent sexual assault
- Public humiliation or rejection
- Rejection and/or abandonment by someone to whom you have revealed your inner self
- Suicide by someone close to you
  You may assume that you must not be worth living for, assuming that if you were a worthwhile person the loved one would have chosen to go on living.
- Loss of a job, especially when the displacement is justified by pointing out something wrong with you that you cannot change such as you are too old, incapable of handling the work, and so on
- Having something terrible happen at an early age, such as the death of a close loved one, divorce of parents, severe physical injury or handicap, and so on
  You conclude there must be something wrong with you since children tend to believe bad things happen to bad people.

PERSONAL EVALUATION

Consider each category, and note anything that comes to mind about possible sources of the shame that inhibits your life. Pay particular attention to the one area of shame you are working on during your 30-day journey.

ACTION

Make three lists citing what you think may be the sources of shame in your life from each of the three categories: shame assigned to you by others, shame derived from chronic exposure to a shameful environment, and shame resulting from an isolated branding experience.

REFLECTION

You are not bound up by shame unless there are specific sources of your shame. How might re-examining the sources of your shame as an adult give you a new perspective on the conclusions you drew about yourself at an earlier age?

ENCOURAGEMENT

Once you identify the sources of your shame, you will be able to identify resources to help you deal with each one, finding healing for the brokenness and a new perspective that can free you from the bonds of shame.

Discovering Resources to Help You

Once you have identified the suspected sources of your shame, you can actively discover and gain access to resources to help you reduce the power that shame has over you. Each particular source of shame needs to be treated appropriately. If you fail to diagnose the sources of shame and deal with them according to their kind, you may waste your energy trying to stop the symptoms without ever getting to the root of the problem. If you identify the source and find resources to deal with the root issues, you will eliminate the symptoms as the result of eliminating the source of the symptoms.

For shame that has been assigned to you by others, you need to assess your beliefs about yourself, evaluate who and what convinced you of these beliefs, and challenge them to change them.

For shame that has resulted from chronic exposure to a shameful environment, you need to stop running from the pain of what happened to you and around you so that you can gain a new perspective on what the past experiences truly mean about you. If the chronically shameful circumstances involved abuse, failings, or shameful behavior in the lives of your parents, it is normal as a child to absolve them and take the blame on yourself. Now, as an adult, you have the power to reinterpret the events of childhood with a broader perspective.

If your shame originated with an isolated branding experience, you need to find some way to regain the power you lost, to understand what allowed you to be vulnerable to that type of experience, to take steps to protect yourself from experiencing something similar again, to make whatever amends are necessary, to find a place of support and healing for the emotional injuries that occurred, and to pick up the pieces of your life and find a way to go forward to a better future.

You can look several places for the resources you need:

1. Yourself: personal resources of intellect, energy, determination, courage, and the like
2. Skills you can learn to help you live and think differently
3. Knowledge that will give you a new perspective
4. Individuals who will lend support to your efforts
5. Groups that counteract your shame
6. Organizations designed specifically to cope with issues related to the sources of your shame
7. God, who is committed to seeing you experience freedom to become all He intended you to become

PERSONAL EVALUATION

Look at the lists you made yesterday citing the sources of your shame, and select one source of shame from each of the three categories.

Across the top of a sheet of paper, list the source of your shame you have selected to work on. (You will need a separate sheet for each of the three categories.) Down the length of the paper, list the seven categories of possible resources, then brainstorm and research the resources available to deal with your particular source of shame. List all that you find under the appropriate category.

Here are the steps to finding resources in any area of interest.

Step One   Identify the area where you need help or more information. (You have already done this.)

Step Two   Check at your local library for books on the topic or related topics. Use the card catalog. Ask a librarian to recommend some books on the topic or guide you to the section of the library that holds the books you need.

Step Three   Contact organizations that are set up to deal with issues related to your area of interest.

- Another way to track down groups and organizations is to use your telephone directory. Look under city, county, state, and federal governments for numbers of agencies. If you are not sure that a particular agency can help you, call and explain what information or help you are trying to locate. Staff persons will usually know where to direct you if they cannot help you.

· Consider the growing network of treatment centers and recovery groups.

ACTION

When you finish brainstorming on your own or with your companion, do research to locate specific resources that are within your reach logistically and financially. If you feel uncomfortable talking to someone and admitting that you need help in this area of shame, it is OK to have your companion help or make phone calls so that you remain anonymous.

Take action today to access at least one resource in each category. Get your hands on the resource, use the resource, or make a committed appointment to gain access to the resource within the next week. Ask your companion to hold you accountable to use these resources to move toward reaching the goals you established on Day 7.

ENCOURAGEMENT

Tremendous resources within your reach will help you gain freedom from shame. As you discover and access these resources, you will find the power that will help you break free into a new life.

Establishing a Support Network

The path of shame is trodden in isolation as you try to keep your distance from others as a means of self-protection. The path leading to freedom from shame cannot be walked alone. You must find the courage and reach out to some select individuals and groups who can become a support network.

Your support network may include the following:

- A few friends whose involvement in your life goes beyond helping you work through your issues of shame

  In these relationships you are accepted as you are, you are free to share honestly about the struggles you are working through without having to fear rejection, and you also learn to give of yourself to them so that the friendship is not one-sided. These people should share common interests and values.
- A support group whose involvement in your life is primarily focused on dealing with issues related to your sources of shame

  You may want to create a group brought together in response to your specific need. Or you may want to join a group already in existence that is dealing with issues related to your area of shame.

- A qualified counselor or therapist who has successful experience helping others work through shame-related issues similar to yours
- The staff of a hospital treatment program with a successful track record of helping people recover from the shame-related issues you are dealing with
- Mentors who can become positive role models as you move out of shame and toward a healthier self-image and healthier way of life
- Spiritual support persons who are willing to commit themselves to help you find and experience the love and grace of God in a nonshaming way

PERSONAL EVALUATION

- Do you already know people who may have the qualities needed to be supportive as you move toward freedom from shame? Jot down a list of the twenty most likely people. You will draw from this list later.
- What support groups, recovery organizations, treatment centers, church groups, and so on did you discover from your previous research that might be of support to you?
- What qualified counselors and/or treatment programs in your area deal with the issues you face?
- Can you name people you would like to have as mentors?

ACTION

For this step you will probably need to draw on the strength and encouragement of your companion for this journey. It is understandably difficult for anyone who is bound by shame to reach out and try to assemble a support network.

1. Decide what you need from people before you approach them to be a part of your support network. If you know precisely the extent of the commitment you are looking for and the depth of the relationship you are seeking, it will be easier for them to make a decision about whether they can make that kind of commitment.

2. Talk to several people so that you are not devastated when some decline to be a part of your support network.

3. Have someone hold your hand and hold you accountable to keep working at establishing a support network until all the pieces are in place.

4. Replace people who drop out or don't work out in terms of being supportive. You won't find the perfect mix immediately. This is a process of trial and error; however, the error does not have to be taken to mean that there is something wrong with you or that there is something wrong with them.

Complete the following goal sheet for establishing your support network. Include only those you need.

GOAL SHEET

- The friends I have found to fill this need are

  —————————————————————————.

- My support group is made up of

  —————————————————————————.

- My treatment/recovery program I am involved in is

  —————————————————————————.

- My therapist/counselor is

  —————————————————————————.

- The person I can call when I am in trouble and need to talk openly is

  —————————————————————————.

- My spiritual support persons are

  —————————————————————————.

- My mentors are

  —————————————————————————.

Share this goal sheet with someone today; commit yourself to work on establishing a support network until the sheet is complete, and ask the person to hold you accountable.

REFLECTION

Consider which person or group would be easiest for you to approach as a first step in establishing your support network. When you establish that source of support, you can get help to find the courage to complete the network.

ENCOURAGEMENT

You may be surprised at how many people care about you and want to help. You may also be surprised to find that the people who open their lives to support you are dealing with their own issues and will be helped themselves by being supportive of you.

FOOD FOR THOUGHT

There is nothing so moving—not even acts of love or hate—as the discovery that one is not alone.
—Robert Ardrey

Choosing Someone You Can Safely Tell Your Secrets

Secrecy locks you into your shame. At some point you will need to safely tell your secrets to someone. Becoming honest with yourself, God, and another human being is one of the most powerful things you can do to free yourself from shame. It is also the most powerfully dangerous thing you can do. You live in fear of the devastation you would experience if anyone knew the whole truth about the parts of your life that are kept hidden. If you dare to tell your secrets or reveal yourself to some one who does not respect the importance of the revelation, someone who rejects you, or someone who takes the secrets you share and uses them to publicly humiliate you, the results can be utterly devastating. If the person you confide in does not cover your shame, the individual can compound it when your worst fears are realized. For these reasons you must take the utmost care to find someone who is safe to tell your secrets.

Here are some qualities you will need to find in the people you consider confiding in:

- Humility: understand their own frailty; have gone through their own share of pain with their eyes open and have experienced coming out on the other side of the valley of shame
- Accepting of others: accept themselves and oth-

ers as being subject to human weakness; do not gossip about, crucify, or vilify those who admit the darkness within themselves
- Compassion: empathize with your weaknesses because they recognize that we all have human frailties
- Nonjudgmental: accept you and love you even if they do not approve of some things you have done or been involved in
- Good listener: listen and allow you to express honest feelings and confused ideas without condemning you
- Consistent: can be depended on to be fairly stable at a time when you may be unstable
- Truthful: remind you of the truth and act as a balance to point you back toward reality when you are not seeing life clearly
- Faithful: keep your confidences
- Nothing to gain: do not have a personal interest in your image or how quickly you work through the issues of your shame
- Nothing to lose: have not been personally violated by the secret information or behavior you need to confide
- Encouraging: can see beyond where you are and who you see yourself to be today and can point you in that direction
- Available: can and will make themselves available to you to a reasonable degree

When you feel able to unburden your soul and share the secrets weighing you down with shame, start with someone who is legally or morally bound to keep your confidence. A licensed therapist is bound by law to keep your confidence. A member of the clergy adheres to confidentiality as a strict practice of the moral code.

You may be inclined to confide in your spouse, but you wonder if that is a wise move. Ideally, you should be able to confide in and trust your spouse to protect you, accept you, and love you for better or for worse. Since we don't live in an ideal world and shame-based relationships are often abusive and destructive, carefully consider at what point and at what pace to reveal your shameful secrets to your spouse. It will be helpful if your spouse begins to understand issues related to your areas of shame as preparation for being able to handle your secrets well. If your secret life is markedly different from the person your spouse knows, if you have done things that violate your marriage, or if your spouse has a history of using things you share as ammunition against you, be especially cautious. At some point in your recovery you do need to become honest and open in your marriage. You may need the assistance of a qualified marriage counselor.

PERSONAL EVALUATION

- Do you have secrets that you have never told anyone?
- Do you fear that if others know your secrets, they will reject you and/or humiliate you?

• Who can you trust to keep your confidence when you decide to open up and tell someone your secrets?

ACTION

You may not be ready to reveal your secrets to someone yet. That is OK. Today make a list of three people to tell when you feel ready.

REFLECTION

• What is your emotional reaction when you consider the possibility of telling someone your secrets?
• What do you fear will happen?

ENCOURAGEMENT

There is tremendous relief when you finally unburden yourself of the weight of your secrets and find acceptance instead of humiliation. I encourage you to find someone who is safe, then dare to unlock the chains of your shame by sharing your secrets with another human being.

FOOD FOR THOUGHT

We are only as sick as the secrets we keep.
—Anonymous

Considering a Change of Location

Sometimes a change of location can be helpful in your journey toward freedom from shame. If your shame is assigned to you by others, it can be helpful to have some distance from the people who continually heap shame on you. If your shame is related to chronic conditions in your environment or ongoing violations of your personal boundaries, it can be helpful to set up a new living situation where the sources of shame are reduced.

A change of location will not eliminate your shame. Shame is something you carry with you in your view of yourself. But a change of location can give you rest from the accumulation or aggravation of shame so that you can begin to deal with the issues within you.

When considering a change of location, you must balance the advantages of making such a move with the other factors in your life. You need to consider

- the effect a move would have on your family.
- whether you are running away so that you can deal with the issues related to your shame or you are running away so that you don't have to face and deal with them.
- what you will be giving up in terms of a support

network available in your current location and how you plan to replace that support network in a new location.

- practical matters such as having a place to live, a comparable job, and so on.

PERSONAL EVALUATION

- Do you believe that a change of location could be helpful in reducing the accumulation and aggravation of shame in your life?
- Are you telling yourself that a change of location will make your shame go away? (It won't.)
- Where would you go if you were to consider a change of location?
- How would such a move affect your family members at this stage of their lives?
- Are you running away so that you can deal with the issues related to your shame, or are you running away so that you can escape dealing with the issues related to your shame?
- What would you be losing in terms of a support network?
- What is available in the new location that could replace the support network you would give up by moving?
- How would you go about establishing a support network in your new location?
- What are the practical realities you would need to consider? Could you and working family members find comparable employment? What

about schools? Child care? Is the cost of living manageable? Is there a community where the needs of your family would be adequately met?

ACTION

On a sheet of paper list all the advantages from making a change of location on one side and all the disadvantages on the other. Ask your family members who are old enough to participate in family meetings to do the same from their perspective. Discuss the possibilities, and come to a decision that will best meet the needs of your family. Remember, whatever you decide today doesn't have to be a decision to live in another location for the rest of your days.

REFLECTION

In your heart of hearts, with all things considered, what do you feel would be most beneficial to your well-being and the well-being of your family: staying where you are and working through the shame in familiar surroundings, or moving to a new location to work through your shame?

Limiting the Influence of People Who Shame You

Shame does not become unhealthy until you accept the conclusion that whatever is being said or done truly means something shameful about you. You can learn to limit the influence of people in your life who shame you without changing them. People around you may continue to spew out potentially shame-producing words, attitudes, and behavior, but you can learn to stop the influence before it reaches your heart. Here are several ways to limit the influence of people who shame you:

1. Limit your exposure to them. Limit your involvement with people who see you in a negative light, who reinforce your shameful view of yourself, who expect the least of you, who criticize and tear you down. You cannot make them change, but you can choose to weigh the effects of their shameful ways on you and decide not to be around them as much.

The truth is, no other person will be able to deem you an acceptable human being. Freedom from shame is found by learning to appreciate your unique value apart from others' pronouncements about you or their opinions of you. One step in this direction is to let go of damaging relationships and limit your exposure to people who treat you shamefully.

2. Counterbalance the shame others try to place on you. Sometimes people will tell you that problems and conflicts in your relationship are precipitated because something is wrong with you. Condemning statements like, "If you were more of a man (woman), our marriage wouldn't be in trouble," or "You are utterly selfish," may cause you to doubt yourself.

Don't accept these shaming attacks on your personal identity without a challenge. Confront the condemnation and conclude that the person is wrong about you. Counterbalance the attack with the perspective of someone else who sees you in a more positive light. The next time an attack of this kind occurs, don't fight with the person hurling the condemnation. Instead call a friend, explain what was said, and describe how the confrontation caused you to feel. After you have dealt with some of your feelings, ask your friend to help you counterbalance this dark view of yourself with positive things in your life.

3. Refuse to dance. Often in shame-based relationships one person manipulates the other by using condemnation to get the other to do what he wants or to conform to the role she wants the other to play. You are being manipulated with condemnation whenever the other person suggests that you need to be more, better, or different than you are. The moment you respond directly to the condemnation by trying to do something to prove the person is wrong or by trying to change to get

the person to change the opinion of you, you have joined the dance.

You refuse to dance when you objectively determine that you have not done anything wrong and refuse to respond to the condemnation. Instead calmly, but firmly, explain that you don't accept the estimation of you, you are sorry the person thinks you should be different, but you refuse to be manipulated into trying to change who you are to please him.

4. Learn to freeze the frame and take time out. Whenever people treat you shamefully, stop the action in your mind. Take a moment to emotionally step back from the situation; consider what their behavior and attitude mean about them, not just what they mean about you. Oftentimes you will be able to see that their poor behavior reflects their own insecurities, hurts, and fears. If you see that other people may feel as hurt and scared inside as you do, you will not necessarily accept their potentially shameful behavior as evidence there is something wrong with you.

PERSONAL EVALUATION

- In which relationships would limiting your exposure to the other person be a good way to limit the shameful influence in your life?
- Who can you call on to counterbalance condemnation and shame when they are assigned to you?
- Which relationships in your life are character-

ized by being drawn into a dance that ends up causing you to feel shamed?

- Take a moment to think about the people in your life who shame you. What might their behavior say about their own insecurities, problems, hurts, or fears that have nothing to do with you?

ACTION

Call someone in your support network and explain the ways you are learning to limit the influence of the people who shame you. Ask the person to give you feedback and help you learn to practice these new ways of relating. The next time someone behaves in a way that invites you to accept shame, call your support person and talk it over.

REFLECTION

Recall a situation where someone did something that you allowed to produce shame within you. Now imagine three or four different ways that you could limit the shame you accept by using the advice given in today's journey.

ENCOURAGEMENT

As you practice these relational skills, you will begin to enjoy a sense of power that comes when you realize you can limit the influence of people who shame you.

Drawing Close to Those Who Cover Your Shame

As a child, Karen went without shoes most of the time. When school was in session, she was often ashamed of the hand-me-down shoes her parents made her wear. Many times she hid her feet under the desk in hopes the other children wouldn't notice how outdated and marred her shoes were. Sometimes she succeeded. Other times her peers delighted themselves by teasing her about her shoes. Karen never told anyone what happened. It seemed ridiculous, especially because such a little thing was a powerful source of shame for her.

Karen had forgotten all about it until a moment came when the shame of her childhood was rekindled. Karen and her husband both lost their jobs suddenly and unexpectedly when she was five months pregnant. She didn't even try to find a new job until after the baby came. Her husband was unable to find employment for several months, although he sought work diligently. Eventually, their finances dwindled to almost nothing, the baby was nearly due, and Karen was sinking into depression.

The night before Easter, Karen was trying to find something decent to wear to church but wasn't having much luck because her body and feet had swollen out of proportion to her clothes and shoes.

The only nice dress that fit had a stain on it, and the only shoes she could squeeze her feet into were badly worn. Karen's friend Sue was visiting that evening. When Karen came out of the bedroom to see if her outfit was passable, she was in no mood to handle criticism. Not realizing how badly Karen was feeling about herself, her husband blurted out, "You can't wear those shoes. They look awful." Karen burst into tears. The pain of her childhood shame came rushing in on her. She relived the feelings of shame she had known when she tried to hide her feet under the desk so no one would notice the symbol of her poverty.

After a few moments Karen gained her composure. Sue asked if she would mind coming with her on some errands, and Karen agreed. The first stop Sue made was at a shoe store where she sat her friend down and helped her select a pair of new white shoes that fit. At church the next day Karen didn't have to hide her feet because she had a friend who knew how to cover her shame without making her feel like a charity case.

A person who covers your shame is someone who

- sees beyond the circumstances and garb of the moment to the beauty within you.
- understands the pain and humiliation associated with your shame and takes action to relieve the pain and protect you from humiliation.
- is in a position to help you cover or replace some of the things that symbolize your shame, those

things that cause you to lower your head, fear exposure, and feel ashamed of yourself.
- loves you enough to help you see yourself in a new light.

PERSONAL EVALUATION

Cinderella's fairy godmother covered the rags of shame Cinderella was dressed in and actually helped her see herself differently so that she could go where she wanted to go and do what she wanted to do.

- Is there someone who sees beyond the circumstance and soil to envision what you can become, recognizes the wonder of you, acknowledges your unique talents, affirms your value, and encourages you that you have what it takes to make it in this world?
- Who can help you bridge the gap between where you are and where you want to be?
- Who can cover your shame and treat you with respect?
- Can you think of an incident when someone treated you with kindness and respect and lessened your sense of shame?

ACTION

Make a conscious decision to draw near the people you believe have the love and respect for you that may help you cover the symbols of your shame.

Call one or more of these people and make arrangements to spend some time together next week.

If you can recall specific incidents where others' kindness and respect for you helped you feel better about yourself, call them or drop them a note to express your appreciation.

REFLECTION

Imagine that someone could instantly cover the symbols of your shame. What would she change to help you see yourself differently?

ENCOURAGEMENT

When you cover and replace the symbols of your shame, you will be able to see yourself differently, and others will respond to you in a more accepting way.

FOOD FOR THOUGHT

Dry those tears—you can't go to the ball looking like that.
                    —The fairy godmother to Cinderella

Avoiding Negative Religion, Accepting God's Covering

Negative religion, which plays on your sense of shame to manipulate you into submission, is very damaging. When you already feel that you are terribly flawed, being scolded or harangued in the name of God does nothing to draw you nearer to God or to help you escape your torment. Negative religion can play a role in keeping you in bondage to shame. That is the opposite of what God desires for you.

From beginning to end, the Bible reveals God's plan to free you from the bondage of shame. In the opening chapters man and woman are naked and unashamed. With the fall of humankind, shame enters the world, and God goes to work devising a plan to cover the nakedness, which keeps you in hiding from yourself, others, and God. The prophet Isaiah proclaims the desire of God's heart when he says, "Instead of your shame you shall have double honor, / And instead of confusion they shall rejoice in their portion" (Isa. 61:7).

When Jesus came to earth as a child, God identified with your shame. Jesus was born under the shadow of reproach because His mother was not married when she became pregnant. As a man, He was continually reprimanded by religious leaders because He associated with a shameful lot of char-

acters, most notably prostitutes and societal out-
casts. When He died on the cross, He took on the
sins and the shame of the whole world. He was
mocked, hated, spat upon, stripped before the
gawking eyes of a jeering mob, ridiculed, rejected,
tormented, and left to die because of who He was,
not because of something He had done.

The writer to the Hebrews says that Jesus "en-
dured the cross, despising the shame." He died in
humiliation and nakedness so that He could pur-
chase robes of righteousness to cover your shame
when you stand before God the Father. The apostle
John tells believers to "abide in Him, that when
He appears, we may have confidence and not be
ashamed before Him at His coming" (1 John 2:28).
Jesus Himself is quoted in the last book of the Bible: "Blessed is he who watches, and keeps his gar-
ments, lest he walk naked and they see his shame"
(Rev. 16:15).

God has gone to great lengths to communicate
His unconditional love by identifying with you in
your shame, offering to cover your shame and pro-
viding a remedy for the shame at the core of your
being. It is a terrible tragedy when people who represent God communicate the message in a way
that exposes your shame instead of covering it.
You might have experienced rejection from those
who represent God and turned away from their
negative religion out of a desire for protection and
a justified sense of healthy shame that warned you
to protect your boundaries. Avoiding negative religion is wise, but if you also avoid a relationship

with God, you are cutting yourself off from your most powerful ally in the struggle to find freedom from shame.

Your unhealthy shame may be clouding your interpretation of what is being said and done in the name of God. The real reason you may draw away from God may have little to do with the practice of negative religion. Your inner shame may make you feel certain of God's rejection, and you dare not put yourself in a position of having your fears confirmed.

You may say you have a relationship with God that is private, not including other people. If that is the case, shame still has a strong hold on your spiritual life. The covering God provided for your sin and shame in the form of the cross makes two bridges. One part of the cross was vertical, making a way for relationship with God. The other part of the cross was horizontal, a bridge of restored relationships with others here on earth. God says that a healthy relationship with Him will restore your ability to love and have relationships with others.

Get away from negative religion that uses shame as a tool to keep you in submission, but don't run away from God. Continue to seek God. Look for a community of believers who understand and communicate God's grace and unconditional love. Find a place where God's mercy is celebrated, where the joy of worship comes from understanding God's everlasting love that cannot be vanquished by our humanity.

Here are the elements of healthy nonshaming religion:

- Truth is not compromised on moral standards: right and wrong are clearly upheld but always in the context of God's unconditional love and willingness to forgive you and cleanse you from all sin.
- When sin is acknowledged, confessed to God, and turned from, it is covered rather than publicly exposed.
- Your standing with God is on the basis of God's grace (unearned favor), not on your performance.
- All people are accepted equally without regard to their outward appearance, worldly status, or wealth.

PERSONAL EVALUATION

- How has negative religion exposed or aggravated your sense of shame?
- Have you ever entered into a relationship with God by trusting Christ's death on the cross to cover your sins?
- Have you ever thought of Jesus as someone who understands your shame, identifies with you in your shame, and wants to cover your shame?
- Is your avoidance of negative religion keeping you from a positive relationship with God?
- Are you willing to keep seeking until you find a community of people who communicate God's

love and grace in a way that helps you find freedom from shame?

ACTION

Ask God to help you find your way beyond any shame associated with negative religion so that you can receive His guidance in gaining freedom from shame.

REFLECTION

- If God is willing to cover your spiritual nakedness so that you can stand before Him unashamed, are you willing to receive the covering He offers you?
- If you were to stand before Him now, do you think you would be covered?

ENCOURAGEMENT

God knows you as you are and chooses to love you anyway.

FOOD FOR THOUGHT

Do not fear, for you will not be ashamed;
Neither be disgraced, for you will not be put to shame;
For you will forget the shame of your youth.
—Isaiah the Prophet

Practice Playing to a New Audience

One high-school football team consistently lost every game they played away from their home stadium. When they played before a supportive audience of friends and family, they played well, maintained a positive attitude in spite of temporary setbacks, and invariably won the game. When they played before a crowd cheering for the other team, they became self-conscious, focusing on what they did wrong, fearing the humiliation they would experience if they lost, anticipating what might go wrong. The predictable reaction of a crowd that was against them caused them to hesitate and lose the game.

Their coach recognized the pattern and devised a solution that allowed them to begin winning games even when they were before a nonsupportive audience. He videotaped every game and reviewed the tape with the team. During the review, he pointed out everything the players did that was right as individuals and as a team. He made corrections as necessary, but the primary focus was on affirming and accentuating the positive. Once the players began to anticipate the postgame reviews, they began playing to a new audience; they were playing to their coach and to themselves. They knew what made for success in the game and what they would be proud of in the coming review. When they learned to play to the new audience, their performance at away games improved dramatically and became more consistent.

When you live with an unhealthy sense of shame, you carry an imaginary audience with you. In your mind, people around you are looking down on you, expecting poor performance, and waiting for the opportunity to humiliate you. You feel self-conscious of your flaws. Seeing yourself as a loser in the game of life, you dread the mistakes you are sure you will make. When you do stumble or make an error, you are sure that people are watching and demeaning you as a result.

Imagining this type of negative audience is a common experience for most adolescents. However, if people develop a clear sense of personal identity and positive self-regard during the maturing process, they move beyond carrying a negative imaginary audience with them. People with unhealthy shame often don't move beyond the juvenile struggle to establish a positive personal identity. Shame is often related to symptoms of arrested development and immature behavior. As long as you continue to play to a negative audience that you imagine to be watching every move and waiting to pounce on any flaw, you will be unable to consistently do your best and win at the game of life.

Begin playing to a new audience. First, do what you can to get rid of the negative audience. If some people in your life seem to be cheering against you, remove yourself from them and their critique as much as you can. If your shame is related to an experience of public exposure and people know intimate details of your life that are shameful, remove yourself from the community for a while if possible; give yourself time to recover enough from the devastation to be less dramatically affected by the attitudes and reactions of others. If you are in a community where your reputation is a point of shame for you, consider moving away from the gaze of a community that will continue to see you in a shameful light and reflect a negative image.

Find a place where people view you with a fresh perspective or see your positive qualities. You could discover a new location or a group within your present location where you can relate to people in terms of your positive qualities. Perhaps it is a class in a subject you do well in, a job setting where you can use your abilities to make a good impression, or a volunteer situation where you do something helpful and productive for others. Enjoy the positive feedback you receive. Do not feel obligated to cue them in to the fact that the positive side they are seeing is not the whole picture.

Include the supportive eyes of God in your audience in much the same way the high-school football team included the supportive gaze of their coach in their new audience. Remind yourself that God is on your side. Even though you cannot see Him, He always has His eyes on you and cheers for you.

PERSONAL EVALUATION

- Do you tend to carry around a negative or supportive imaginary audience? How does that affect your performance in life?
- What can you do to limit or get rid of the real negative audience that may be a source of ongoing criticism and shame?
- What can you do to find a place where you are playing before a supportive audience?
- Are you willing to believe that God is watching you with positive regard and high hopes for your success? How would your life be different if you could really believe this?

ACTION

Decide one thing you can do today to limit your exposure to a negative audience. Do that one thing.

Select one way you can find a positive audience, and take a step toward placing yourself in that setting. Choosing something related to the specific area of shame you are focusing on during your journey is best.

Pray and ask God to help you see Him on your side.

ENCOURAGEMENT

You are probably much harder on yourself in your own mind than others are in real life. You can learn to see yourself in a more positive light.

Change Your Mind to Change Your Life

Research has shown that your mind will cling to foundational beliefs and throw out any new ideas that disagree with your preconceived ideas, even if your beliefs are not based on truth. If you see yourself as ugly and someone offers you a compliment about your appearance, you automatically dismiss the possibility that the compliment is genuine. Instead you wonder what he wants from you, why he is teasing you, or what is wrong with him that he can't see how ugly you are.

To change your mind, you must first acknowledge the foundational beliefs. Look carefully at your negative beliefs about yourself and your negative prophecies about your life. Your negative beliefs would be statements about your identity: "I am a loser"; "I am nothing but trouble"; "I am stupid"; "I am a misfit"; "I am a burden to my loved ones"; and so on. Negative self-prophecies would be the conclusions you draw about life because of negative beliefs about yourself: "I'll never make anything of myself"; "I'll never have a respectable career"; "I'll never be able to provide for my family"; "I'll never marry again because it would just be a disaster"; "I'll never be at a normal weight"; and so on.

Second, challenge your beliefs. Accept the possibility, however slight, that you may be wrong in your self-condemnation.

Third, introduce new evidence that may help you arrive at a new set of beliefs. Accumulate evidence that does not fit with your shameful image of yourself. Notice your good qualities that you have previously discounted. Notice what others say they appreciate about you that you have refused to accept.

Fourth, learn to reinterpret the current and historical facts of your life in a new way. Introduce a new theory about your life and yourself that leaves room for the belief that you may be capable, worthwhile, valuable, and acceptable. In examining the current circumstances of your life, look for explanations for problems that go beyond the assumption that you are deficient in a particular area. In dealing with your history, look for explanations of what happened other than the explanation that people with deficiencies like yours cause or deserve such things to happen to them.

Fifth, change the way you talk to yourself and about yourself in your mind. Open your mind to the hope and possibility that you have been too hard on yourself. Say things like, "I can learn some things"; "I can look nice when I dress up"; "Maybe there is a way I can learn to be productive in one area of my life"; "Maybe I can learn to have a healthy relationship with this person"; "I may be able to find someone who can see some good in me and accept me, maybe even love me"; "I may be able to find a plan I can follow to help me lose weight"; and so on.

PERSONAL EVALUATION

· What negative foundational beliefs do you hold about yourself?
· What negative self-prophecies do you pronounce about your life?
· Can you accept the possibility that you may be wrong about yourself?

ACTION

List three beliefs you hold about the kind of person you are. These statements describe your view of your identity. Focus particular attention on the names you call yourself and the way you see yourself in the area of shame you are working to free yourself from during this journey. *(I am a slob.)*

List three prophetic pronouncements you make about your life and future based on the three beliefs listed above. *(Because I am a slob, I will never have a nice home.)*

Challenge each belief and prophecy in writing by filling in the following statement: Maybe I am not a _____. Maybe there are other explanations for the evidence I interpret in this way. Maybe I can break free to _____ *(do whatever it is the prophetic pronouncement says is off-limits to the kind of person I have labeled myself to be).*

Consider your life. Look for evidence that does not fit with the conclusions you have drawn about yourself. Look at your current facts of life, and reevaluate your history.

List other possible theories about why you appear to be the kind of person you see yourself to be. *(I see myself as a slob because I never learned the basic skills to organize and maintain a clean home.)*

List other possible theories to explain why the bad things in your history happened. Look at what was happening in the lives of others and their state of well-being at the time. Write out your new considerations of how the events may say more about others than they say about you.

Change your life today in some small way that defies your core belief in the area of deficiency you are working on. If you have focused on the belief that you are a slob, get up and clean your kitchen, or clean out your car and wash it until it sparkles.

REFLECTION

Allow yourself to reflect on how different life can be once you learn to change your mind.

ENCOURAGEMENT

You can change the way you see yourself, and in so doing you will be free to change your life.

Look for Seeds of Potential

Everyone has seeds of potential greatness. To produce fruit, you must plant the seed, nourish it, allow time for it to grow, and protect and tend the plant until you see the fruit mature. If any seeds are not recognized for what they are and are therefore never planted, nourished, allowed time to grow, and protected and tended during the growth process, they will never produce the fruit they were created to produce.

Shame tells you there are no seeds of greatness within you, only the dirt! If you believe this about yourself, you will not take the steps necessary to grow the seeds of greatness into the mature fruit of accomplishment. You might have discounted the seeds of potential in your life because someone told you nothing was there or because you compared the tiny seeds in your life with the fully mature fruit in the lives of others and concluded you couldn't measure up. Next to a juicy apple, a little brown apple seed appears pitifully small. If you somehow missed the concept that you have to grow and develop the seeds within you before you taste the good fruit in life, you might have given up before you ever had a chance to see the good within you grow to fruition.

Shame tells you that being different is bad. Each

seed will produce fruit according to its own kind. You might have neglected the seeds in your life because they were different from those around you. For people who are not shamed, being rare and different can be appreciated as marks of increased value. However, when you are in shame, being different is seen in a negative light, proving that you are a misfit or an oddball rather than a special and uniquely valuable person. In gaining freedom from shame, you may need to learn to accept your unique differences and see the good in them.

You may falsely believe that people enjoying the fruits of life you desire have somehow magically acquired their lives because they are fundamentally different from you. Shame may lead you to believe there are two kinds of people: the winners and the losers. But people who have not been held back by shame have nurtured and cared for their seeds of potential throughout their lives. They have recognized their potential, done things that brought growth, and allowed themselves time to develop. Shame might have caused you to neglect nourishing and caring for your seeds of potential and left you without much of a positive nature to show for your life. So the primary difference that sets you apart from persons you envy is the negative effects of shame, not your lack of potential or a fundamental difference between you and them.

When you believe that you were born to lose, you cut yourself off from doing those things that bring your seeds of potential to fruition. Instead you expend your energy in envy, jealousy, covetousness, resentment, and anger over life's unfairness. This belief system is utterly defeating and imprisoning because it says that by some flip of a cosmic coin, others were blessed with what it takes to make it but you were not. This belief system closes the door to future possibilities since there is nothing you can do to change the person you are and move toward the life you desire. In this way shame can lead to antisocial attitudes and actions that further isolate you from the very people who could help you learn how to develop your seeds of potential.

PERSONAL EVALUATION

- What seeds of potential have you taken the time, effort, and energy to nourish and tend over the course of time to develop to fruition?
- Look for the little seeds. Do you have any good qualities you can think of? Have you ever been honest, friendly, kind, or trustworthy? Have you ever displayed abilities or talents, even as a child?
- Think of one area of life you are working on in this journey. How has shame inhibited you from taking action that would develop the seeds of potential in this area?
- What negative attitudes and painful emotions do you experience as a result of comparing yourself with others and feeling that you are fundamentally less than they are in some way?

ACTION

Look at your life and yourself with the goal of finding a few seeds of potential that have not yet been fully nurtured to fruition. List the good qualities you have exhibited even in the smallest degree, and act on demonstrating one of them in some tangible way today.

Write out what it would mean in your life to take action to develop seeds of potential you have recognized, to make a place for the development of this potential, to make time for the potential to develop.

Construct a time line. Describe how long it would take and what would need to happen to bring one area of potential to fruition so that you enjoy the benefits of a fully developed potential.

Identify the first tangible step toward developing this potential. Take that step today. Commit yourself to continue developing this potential.

REFLECTION

Consider how the tiny seeds of good qualities you noted during your personal evaluation can be increased and demonstrated, even in small measure.

Reflect on how your negative attitudes about yourself influence your view of other people, particularly in terms of sparking envious and resentful feelings. Consider how changing your beliefs about why their lives are different from yours could free you to develop the life you desire.

ENCOURAGEMENT

You are not fundamentally less than other people. Once you learn to recognize and grow the seeds of potential greatness within you, your life will improve dramatically.

FOOD FOR THOUGHT

It is never too late to be what you might have been.
—George Eliot

Acquiring Knowledge and Skills to Help You Fit In

Shame is a social disease that causes you to isolate yourself from others. It makes you ill at ease with individuals and with particular groups in society. In any society certain ways of behaving and relating are commonly held to be acceptable. Certain skills enable persons to fit in to whatever community or society of which they are a part. When you are ashamed of yourself and feel that you don't fit in to society in a meaningful way, you may get caught in a cycle of shame that keeps you from developing the skills you need to be able to fit in to society.

Shame keeps this cycle going because you see your lack of social skills as a reflection of a basic lack within yourself. When you fear being exposed as deficient as a person, you become defensive since the risk of rejection for not knowing certain social skills is increased. Every time you are rejected, you may add it to the evidence you interpret to mean that something is unacceptable or unlovable in who you are. The true message may be that your behavior is socially unacceptable. When you are kept from admitting your ignorance in a particular area, you are barred from gaining the very skills that will help you become more easily accepted by society.

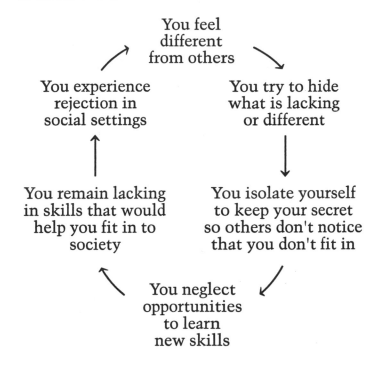

For some people, this cycle is marked by quiet desperation and the lonely hope that no one will notice that they don't fit in. Some people react in anger and rebellion, fighting against the reality that persons must conform to certain societal norms if they expect to be accepted by others. Whatever your emotional response, the fact remains that in a world where you need to get along with other people, you need to learn the skills to do so.

Dare to learn the skills you lack that will help

you fit in to society. Give up your defensive defiance, your retiring helpless position, or your tendency to run away from intimidating situations. The people who function acceptably in society are not better than you; they simply have skills, knowledge, and manners that help them interact successfully with others, which you have not yet acquired. You can learn to change your behavior.

You break the cycle by identifying the skills you lack that trigger shameful feelings and then learning these skills. You will need courage and determination, but you can find ways to learn these skills without having to admit openly that you lack them. In today's world you can learn things and acquire skills in the privacy of your own home. You can use taped seminars, videotapes, computer networking, correspondence courses, books ordered over the phone, and so on.

Review this list of things you can learn and skills you can develop to help you better fit in to society:

- Learn to communicate your ideas and feelings clearly
- Learn manners
- Learn to be a good friend
- Learn to take responsibility for your life (finances, personal grooming, spiritual health, intellectual growth, your home, belongings and so on)
- Learn to give and receive love
- Learn to forgive and accept forgiveness

- Learn a useful occupation
- Learn to responsibly handle your roles in life (wife/husband, mother/father, employer/employee)
- Learn to set and reach personal goals
- Learn to get along with others and maintain relationships

PERSONAL EVALUATION

- What skills do you lack that are a source of shame for you?
- What do you do or exclude yourself from doing in an attempt to keep your lack in this area secret?
- Because of a sense of shame, what opportunities do you refuse or cut yourself off from that could help you develop the skills you need?
- When have you experienced embarrassment or rejection because you remain ignorant or lacking in this way?

ACTION

Choose one skill you lack that is related to the area of shame you are working on during this journey. Find a way you can gain access to the information you need to acquire, and develop this skill without risking shameful exposure.

Nourishing Yourself with Motivational Materials

Andrew lived a double life. To all who knew him in his public life, he was a highly respectable, dedicated family man, a devoted husband, a Christian leader, and a generally nice guy. It was not apparent that Andrew hated himself deeply because of what he believed to be an inescapable flaw in his character, an insatiable lust in his soul, that tore him apart inside. Andrew struggled with a form of sex addiction that went against everything he believed to be right, led him to violate his marriage vows, and left him living in fear and self-loathing while he pretended that everything was fine.

When he could bear the growing weight of shame no longer, he confided to his wife and, later, his pastor the secret life he had been living. The pastor chose to tell other church leaders, and together they chose to make a public example of Andrew. They said that the purpose was to warn others and to have the entire church participate in helping restore him. The results were devastating, leading Andrew to the brink of suicide. Family and friends got him into a treatment program immediately, which stabilized the suicidal reaction. When he completed the program, he had to come home to a community where he was utterly exposed and felt that he would surely drown in shame.

At that point a good friend gave him a set of tapes by Zig Ziglar called *How to Stay Motivated,* including the series *Success and the Self-Image.* In addition to the loving support of family and friends and the timely treatment program, Andrew credits the tapes with literally saving his life and freeing him from shame. In the tapes he first heard the principle: "You are where you are, you are what you are because of what has gone into your mind. You can change where you are, you can change what you are by changing what goes into your mind." The more he listened to the tapes, the more his life began to prove the truth of that principle. As he changed what he put into his mind, he changed where he was in life and even what he was.

Here is what to look for in motivational materials:

- Reality-based message

  Make sure the principles taught respect a healthy sense of your limits. Don't accept things that say you can do anything regardless of your limits. Instead look for materials that say you can do anything within the limits of your physical reality, your family commitments and priorities, moral standards, and so on.
- Consistency with your moral principles and personal values
- Practical application to your life
- Stories that show how people you identify with

as being like you have overcome shame to break free into a new life

Here is how motivational materials can free you from shame:

- They keep you focused on having a positive attitude on a day-to-day basis.
- They counteract the effects of negative criticism. Some psychologists believe that for every criticism you receive, you need nine positive comments or affirmations to counteract its impact. People who live in shame often get an overdose of criticism from negative people and from negative self-criticism. A daily dose of motivational materials can counteract the criticism until it diminishes.
- They skillfully challenge your false foundational beliefs.
- They inspire hope and help you see beyond your walls of shame to envision how good life could be.
- They give you instruction in developing people skills that will help you learn to better fit in to society.

PERSONAL EVALUATION

- Have you ever experienced the positive influence of motivational materials in helping you gain freedom from shame?

- In what ways can you see that you are where you are and what you are because of what has gone into your mind (either a positive or a negative correlation)?
- Are you willing to nourish yourself daily with positive motivational materials? If not, why?

ACTION

Go to your local bookstore or library, and get some positive motivational materials that will counteract the effects of your shame. Begin to feed your mind with what is positive and powerful. As you continue to nourish your mind with motivational materials throughout the remainder of this journey, note their direct effects on where you are and what you are.

REFLECTION

After reading or listening to some positive motivational materials, reflect on how you are affected.

ENCOURAGEMENT

By nourishing your mind with positive input, you are going to see positive results in the form of a better attitude and healthier behavior.

Developing Your Unique Talents and Abilities

Every human being is born with innate talents and abilities that are unique. You do not put in a request for the talents you receive. They are a gift that comes with the package called life chosen for you by your Creator. You simply discover them. One of the best ways to improve your self-image is to develop the talents woven into the fabric of your being.

Expressing a talent is more than something you do; it is an expression of who you are. Therefore, you need to initially express your talents in a protected environment. Venturing to express yourself artistically or creatively and having your artistic expression ridiculed can be a source of further shame.

Marjorie loved to draw from the time she was a small child. She spent hours on end sketching whatever caught her eye. By the time she started school, she was able to draw quite well and gained a sense of healthy pride from positive feedback given by her teachers. When she entered high school, she fell in love with a young man who was artistically gifted and also quite skilled. She took an art class primarily so that she could be near him. Instead of focusing on her unique talent and developing it, she began to compare her work negatively to his. She showed him her work and looked to him for affirmation. When her romantic intentions were rebuffed, she somehow associated the rejection with a lack of appreciation for her talents. Upon leaving high school, she threw away her art supplies and decided that she wasn't particularly talented after all.

Ten years later, a friend mentioned she was taking a painting class and invited Marjorie to join her. The talent was still there. In the supportive environment of a small class Marjorie blossomed. Her paintings were beautiful. Every time she now looks at the lovely paintings exhibited on the walls of her home and prominently displayed in homes of family and friends, she feels a sense of wonder about herself. The expression of her unique talents reminds her that something is quite special about her.

One way to challenge a shameful self-image is to discover and develop your unique talents and abilities. Here are some tips on how to do that in a safe way:

- Find a supportive environment for your artistic or creative expression.
- Don't put yourself in a situation where your creative expression is being graded or compared to that of others.
- Don't use your creative works or expressions to try to gain the approval of someone whose approval you desperately seek.
- Don't show your creative works to people who

have a history of ridiculing you, tearing you down, or criticizing you.
* Find a way to enjoy and appreciate the expression of your talent for the gift that it is.

PERSONAL EVALUATION

* As a child, what did you love to do, have a strong interest in, or display a special ability for (art, drama, athletics, music, mechanics, language)?
* Have you ever experienced rejection or ridicule in the area of your talents and abilities?
* What effect did that have on your willingness to develop and use your talents?
* What effect did that have on your self-image?

ACTION

Identify one talent or ability that you were born with. Make a list of several ways you could develop or use this talent in some form of creative expression. Do some research to identify an outlet for this talent that would fit the criteria as a safe, supportive environment for creative expression. Become involved in using and developing this talent.

REFLECTION

Think of a time when you felt good about yourself as a result of the creative expression of your talents. Allow yourself to recall the scene as vividly as possible. Allow yourself to feel the good feelings associated with this memory.

ENCOURAGEMENT

You are a talented human being. Every time you choose to creatively express your talents, you are compensating for what you have focused on as being shameful and are giving your self-image a legitimate boost.

FOOD FOR THOUGHT

The expression of your unique talents can remind you that there is something wonderfully unique about you.

Finding Fulfillment in Your Work

Your work and your worth are closely related. Shame will affect your feelings about your work, and your feelings about your work will affect your sense of shame. Therefore, you need to find a personally fulfilling occupation and to fulfill the station you hold in your work to the best of your ability. When you are able to reduce the level of unhealthy shame in your life, your performance on the job will be improved. Finding ways to improve your job performance is a practical way to reduce your sense of shame.

Here are some suggestions related to shame and work:

- Try to find an outlet for what you do well in your work.

    When looking for a job, seek a position that calls for the talents, skills, and abilities you have already developed. In whatever job you are doing now, take the initiative and try to find ways your particular abilities and talents can be useful to your employer.
- Try not to lock yourself into a job that symbolizes shame for you (that is, you are embarrassed to tell anyone what you do).

    If you feel trapped in a job that is shameful in

your mind, you will reinforce your shameful self-image every day.

· Try to find a job in a field and a workplace where you will associate with people you can respect.

You may draw a sense of your value from judging yourself by the people you spend time with. Although you want to reach a level of health so that you will not judge yourself in that way, at this point you may need to work with people for whom you maintain a measure of respect.

· Do what you can to achieve measurable goals, and perform in ways that will gain the approval of your supervisor.

You can do little things that will be noticed right away. Arrive for work ten minutes early; offer to take on special projects.

· Doing well in your work and receiving recognition for a job well done will go a long way toward reducing your level of shame.

· Learn to be the best you can be in your job.

Find self-fulfillment in honest work. Even if your present job is not the job you want to be doing long-term, there is no shame in any job done to the best of your ability.

· Don't let your station in life limit your enjoyment of life or define who you are.

You are more than what is represented by your occupation. Learn to see yourself as a whole person who also fulfills some role in society that needs to be done. Affirm yourself for the quality of the job you do and the energy you devote to your work.

- If you know that social status and the economic power associated with a more prestigious career are important to you, make sensible plans to move on to an occupation you consider more fulfilling.

  You are not trapped! Decide what you want to do in the future. Consider your current commitments, and make plans that allow you to continue meeting your present commitments while moving toward your new occupation. It may take several years to make a smooth transition to the career you envision, but if it is an important element in establishing a sense of self-respect, it is worth the studied planning and effort to make the transition.

- Take steps to continue your education in areas that will help you make notable contributions on the job.

  Being able to see tangible evidence that you are a contributing member of the team at work will counteract your feelings of shame.

- Don't hop from job to job, expecting to discover an occupation that will magically make you feel better about yourself or prove your worth in this world.

  Remember, shame can be helped somewhat by external influences, but the primary source of healing for shame-related issues is within you and your choice to fully discover and use your abilities in your current situation.

- Get whatever help is necessary to resolve your conflicts with authority figures.

If you struggle with shame, you probably have difficulties submitting to authority and consistently exercising authority. Problems relating to authority figures tend to relate to the roots of shame and may best be resolved by discussing the issue with a therapist or counseling professional.

PERSONAL EVALUATION

- How does your sense of shame negatively affect your work?
- How does your work affect your sense of shame?
- Does your current job symbolize shame for you? If so, why do you stay? Does your sense of shame make you feel incapable of finding more fulfilling work? What do you think it would take for you to move into a position that is not shameful?
- Are you able to respect the people you associate with at work? If not, how does that affect your sense of self-respect?
- Do you perform your job to the best of your ability?
- If you are dissatisfied with your line of work, what would you like to be doing? Do you have a plan to get from where you are to where you want to be? What is stopping you from devising such a plan?
- What could you do to educate yourself that would be directly applicable to your work?

- Do you have a history of job hopping? How do you think that is related to your sense of shame?
- Do you have recurrent problems relating successfully within structures of authority? If so, are you willing to seek help to resolve these difficulties?

ACTION

Choose one or two ways you can apply the suggestions given relating to your work, and take action to do them.

REFLECTION

Consider specific ways that gaining freedom from shame will help you in your work. Consider what you can do on the job tomorrow that will reduce your sense of shame.

ENCOURAGEMENT

You can make changes in your attitude and actions on the job that will reduce your sense of shame. Do yourself the favor of doing whatever you do to the best of your ability.

FOOD FOR THOUGHT

The contributions you make in your work are valuable, but your value as a human being goes far beyond what you do.

Practice Treating Yourself with Respect

Shame is characterized by a lack of healthy self-respect. Building a sense of self-respect can begin with a choice. When you are shamed, you probably don't feel respectable, at least not in the areas where shame has a hold on you. If you wait until you feel respectable before you practice treating yourself with respect, your life will remain in the rut of shame to which you have become accustomed. If you wait for someone else to treat you with respect, you place yourself in the role of a helpless victim and give up the power you have to change your life. You don't have to wait until you feel valuable and respectable to practice treating yourself and others with respect.

The road to freedom from shame must begin on the firm foundation of what is true about you, not the shifting sands of how you feel about yourself. The truth is that you are a human being, and as a human being, you are valuable. On the basis of this fact, you take a step of faith. You say to yourself, "Because I am a valuable human being, I choose, as an act of my will, to treat myself with respect." Once you practice treating yourself with respect, the feelings will follow. You will begin to feel more respectable.

One benefit of treating yourself and others with

respect is that you discover the power of a trust-worthy principle. You get back in kind and degree what you give. When you treat yourself and others with respect, the feedback you receive from others will generally become more respectful. Since being treated with disrespect can be a source of un-healthy shame, you receive a double benefit by making the choice to practice self-respect: the im-provement in the way you feel about yourself, and the increase in positive feedback from others. Al-though you do not want to base your self-respect solely on the reactions of others, it will prove help-ful in your season of strengthening your self-esteem to have positive feedback from others.

Notice the use of the word *practice* in the pre-ceding paragraphs. You are probably not used to treating yourself with respect. It will take some practice for you to feel comfortable with the new way of treating yourself. That is OK. Don't stop just because treating yourself with respect may feel awkward for a while. These awkward feelings are not generated because you are being a phony by treating yourself respectfully or because you don't deserve to be treated with respect—as you may as-sume. You will feel awkward because this is some-thing new for you, and new things take practice.

Here are some ways you can treat yourself with more respect:

- Keep yourself, your surroundings, and your be-longings clean.
- Establish and maintain order in your life.

- Behave in ways that are socially acceptable; mind your manners.
- Dress up, and groom yourself to look your best.
- Exercise, rest, and eat healthfully.
- Stand up straight, head held high, shoulders back, and smile.
- Protect your privacy.
- Say no when you mean no.
- Practice discretion in your relationships.

  You do not have to explain your whole life story to others. Choose how much of your life you want to reveal at any given moment, and give yourself permission to keep some things to yourself.
- Stop using foul language.
- Stop putting yourself down and making belittling comments about yourself.
- Give yourself some time to enjoy each day and have some fun.
- Bring beauty into your surroundings: buy yourself some flowers, put a fresh coat of paint on your home, redecorate, listen to beautiful music, and so on.
- Set new standards within the family for treating one another with respect. Explain to children what is respectful and disrespectful behavior, then require them to treat others with respect. Practice treating them with respect.
- Do for yourself the things that are lacking related to a source of shame.

  For example, if you are ashamed because your parents never took you to a dentist and your teeth are a mess, make an appointment with a dentist.

· Affirm yourself in the areas where you feel ashamed instead of waiting for someone else to fill this emotional void.

For example, let's suppose your parents wanted a boy, but you were a girl; therefore, your feminine qualities were rejected, and you feel shame associated with your gender. Do things to affirm that part of yourself: buy clothes and accessories that help you feel feminine, treat yourself to a bubble bath, wear jewelry that you associate positively with the part of you that was treated as shameful.

PERSONAL EVALUATION

· Are you willing to practice treating yourself with respect before you feel fully respectable?

· Review the list of ways you can practice treating yourself with respect. For each general category listed, identify a specific way you could apply it in your life.

ACTION

Stop reading and do something this very moment that demonstrates treating yourself with respect.

Put your list of specific ways to treat yourself with respect where you can see it. As you go through the rest of your journey, look at the list each day, and place a star next to any things you did that day.

REFLECTION

Think of times when you were treated respectfully by yourself and others. Remember how good you felt and the effect on your outlook and behavior.

ENCOURAGEMENT

By choosing to treat yourself with respect, you are starting a cycle that will generate power to help you gain freedom from shame.

FOOD FOR THOUGHT

When you sow an action, you reap a habit. Sow a habit, reap a character. Sow a character, reap a destiny.

—Zig Ziglar

Establishing Markers on the Road to Health

As you move away from the bondage of shame and into a new life, set up markers along the way to memorialize your progress on the road to health. Having markers benefits you by giving you tangible evidence that you can change your life, reminding you of lessons you have learned, encouraging you when you grow weary of the journey, helping you keep track of positive changes in the way you see yourself, and letting you know when you are slipping back.

You set up markers by finding a way to commemorate specific turning points in your life; identify events, choices, dates, and so on that mark a change in your attitudes, actions, relationships, or life-style. Some turning points might include the following: your choice to enter a treatment program to deal with addiction or shame-related issues; the day you decided to turn your life over to God; specific steps you took to end your isolation; your decision to confess your secrets to someone you could trust; your decision to cross one of the boundaries imposed by your shame (taking a class that you thought you never could understand, beginning to care for your physical appearance, choosing to commit yourself to an intimate relationship, choosing to be honest with someone, and so on).

Here are some turning points and signs of progress you may want to commemorate by establishing markers in your life:

- Anniversaries of momentous events or occasions

   In many twelve-step groups, recovery is celebrated by giving out pins to mark thirty days of sobriety, sixty days, three months, six months, and yearly anniversaries of when sobriety began. Recognize and celebrate the time that passes from the point of important choices you have made to move toward freedom.

- Lessons learned along the way

   When you learn a significant lesson that helps you change your life, take a moment to write down what you have learned and to share the lesson with someone else. Share the lesson with your children and friends whenever it is appropriate. By sharing the lesson over and over again, you offer help to others, and you remind yourself of an understanding that helps you.

- Commitments you and others have made to one another

   As you gain freedom from shame, you will begin to experience more freedom to establish relationships with others. In building relationships you will learn to establish boundaries, expectations, and commitments. Commitments in your relationships will play a fundamental role in helping you feel safe enough to reveal yourself to those you love and trust. Whenever you enter into relational commitments (to be honest with each other, to ask for what you need, or to marry), make sure the commitment is clearly defined and recognized by both persons. As time passes you can celebrate the anniversaries of commitments that have been kept.

- Deaths to grieve

During the journey of life, there are deaths to grieve. The Bible says that unless a kernel of grain falls to the earth and dies, it will never bring forth fruit. In your life and journey a measure of death will occur so that new life can blossom and grow. Some things you took comfort in as a relief from your shame (even if they were inappropriate) will die a natural death as you move out of shame. Unhealthy relationships you were complacent with won't work anymore if you are moving toward health and the other person is not. Some things in your life will have to be put to death so that you can continue moving toward health. Shameful behaviors, addictions used to medicate the pain of your shameful feelings, and relationships with people who continue to violate your healthy boundaries must be put to death and buried with your past.

Although these deaths occur on the road to a new life and may mark the end of something quite destructive, every death is painful to bear. Allow yourself to appreciate the loss and the pain that comes when you know you can never go back again to that particular experience or relationship. Give yourself permission to grieve the loss before you move on to the new life that awaits you.

· Births

Commemorate every new beginning, every first step, every time you are able to do something that you were once kept from doing by shame and a fear of rejection. As you gain freedom from shame, these emotional snapshots will remind you about how far you have come.

PERSONAL EVALUATION

Go through this list and specify every place you can set up a marker on your road toward health. Include your decision to take this 30-day journey.

ACTION

Draw a time line based on specific dates in your life. Write on it each marker you listed on your personal evaluation.

Share your time line with your companion for this journey or with some other supportive person.

Do something to celebrate the progress you have already made.

REFLECTION

· Have you come farther than you realized?
· In doing your time line, did you realize there are some turning points you need to take soon?
· What might they be?

ENCOURAGEMENT

There is a road of freedom from shame, and you have begun to walk on that road. As you continue moving in the right direction at your own pace, you will arrive at a place of health.

FOOD FOR THOUGHT

Every point of progress deserves its own memorial.

DAY
27

Adopting New Rituals and Symbols

A ritual is a repetitive pattern of behavior that has a special meaning associated with it. All cycles of human behavior involve rituals that can be destructive or life enhancing. If your life is hampered by shame, you probably observe destructive rituals in your behavior, perhaps without recognizing them as such. In any addictive cycle there are rituals that prepare the way for indulging in the addiction: places you go, things you do, and ways of relating to others that become a familiar part of your routine associated with trying to alleviate the pain of life. Rituals are your attempt to bring some order to your life.

When you begin to change your life—drawing away from the old familiar behaviors, relationships, attitudes, and ways of relating—you will necessarily upset old rituals. You will disrupt the familiar pattern of your life that emanated from your unhealthy sense of shame. You will stop going places, doing the things you routinely used to do, and associating with people who trigger your sense of shame. You will break patterns of relating that were dictated by shame.

If you are in recovery from addiction, putting a stop to the rituals associated with your addiction is key to establishing your sobriety. The alcoholic would stop going to the bar on the way home from work; the compulsive overeater would stop having a morning cup of coffee at the donut shop. If one manifestation of your shame was codependent behavior (you neglected your life while trying to control, fix, or change someone else), stopping the destructive rituals in your life would include choosing not to rescue others from the consequences of their problems.

It is not enough to eliminate destructive rituals. You need to adopt new ones that uphold your healthy boundaries and affirm your new way of life. For someone who feels ashamed of living in a messy home, a new ritual may be clearing the table and washing the dishes after every meal. Some other new rituals may include belonging to a twelve-step group or other nonshaming support group, working a twelve-step program, attending classes to further your education, participating in an exercise program, making weekly dates with your spouse, having daily quiet time for reflection and prayer, attending church or other spiritually uplifting services, reading and listening to motivational materials, participating in an outlet for your talent such as joining a theater group or choir, observing daily grooming practices that underscore your commitment to take care of yourself and look your best, reading bedtime stories to your children, having a weekly manicure, volunteering to help in your community, and so on.

You also need to replace old symbols of your shame with new symbols representing your new beliefs about yourself. A symbol is any token you use to represent something or to which you assign significant meaning. If you review the sources of your shame, you will be able to identify those things that have come to be symbols of shame for you. One man who grew up in poverty always associated tea bags with his shame because the family of twelve would have to share one tea bag on cold mornings when there was nothing to eat. For him, a new symbol that signified his distance from poverty was a fresh tea bag with each cup of tea.

PERSONAL EVALUATION

- What are some destructive life patterns and rituals associated with your shame?
- What are some new rituals you could adopt to nurture yourself? Involve having fun and leisure? Center around family life? Enhance committed relationships?
- What are some places that trigger shameful feelings? Are you willing to avoid these places and find new places to go to meet the same needs in healthy ways?
- If you are not sure what patterns of life are destructive, are you willing to work with a qualified counselor to explore the issue?
- What are some things that symbolize your shame?
- What are some things you can assign meaning to so that they symbolize your new beliefs about yourself and your healthier way of life?

ACTION

Select one daily routine and weekly ritual you can commit yourself to practice that will replace the old rituals associated with the area of shame you are working on during this journey. (It is OK if you are already practicing these rituals.)

If you are not already routinely practicing these life-enhancing rituals, commit yourself to do so for the next six weeks, and begin immediately.

REFLECTION

What effect do you see healthy new rituals and new symbols having on your life and self-image?

ENCOURAGEMENT

As you establish and maintain new rituals and symbols, you are doing the best you can do to keep yourself from relapsing into your old way of life.

DAY 28

Planning to Cope with Weaknesses

Everyone has areas of weakness. When you have an unhealthy sense of shame, you are not free to acknowledge your weaknesses because they are seen as proof of your deficiency as a human being. When you see your weaknesses as proof that you are irreparably damaged, you will be immobilized and unmotivated to try to change. Instead you will avoid or disavow your weaknesses. Healthy shame allows you to acknowledge your weaknesses without feeling like a failure as a person. If this journey has helped you to any degree, you will be better able now to acknowledge and cope with your weaknesses in positive ways. You will have greater freedom to take responsibility for your life and act to make improvements in the areas where you are weak.

Here are some things to keep in mind as you make plans to cope with your weaknesses:

1. Look to God to give you strength and to be your strength when you are weak.

2. Be patient with yourself. Growth and lasting change take time. If you are making good choices and doing the little things that will build you up and strengthen you, over the course of time you will see marked improvement. If you demand immediate transformation, you are setting yourself

up for disappointment and may wrongly conclude that you cannot change. The truth is, you can change, but the changes take more time than you expect.

3. Recognize that there are some areas of weakness where you will never be strong and do not need to be. No one is strong on all points. What makes for meaningful relationships is that you learn to love others in a way that allows you to be strong for them where they are weak and allows them to be strong for you where you are weak. Instead of trying to be strong on all points, develop the strengths you already have. Learn to appreciate the strength you see in others without condemning yourself because you are not like them. Remember, they are not strong in all the areas where you are strong.

4. In areas of weakness that are important to you and that negatively affect your ability to successfully relate to God, your family, friends, and society, make a plan to deal with the weaknesses. You can change by learning new things, exercising the things you already know to be good, setting goals and learning to accomplish them. Make the commitment to learn how to set meaningful goals, then set your goals to overcome the effect of your weaknesses.

5. Identify areas of weakness and plan to cope with them one by one rather than all at once. If you are focusing on overcoming an addiction, give yourself some slack on improving your education and keeping your home perfectly in order. If you

are focusing on taking better care of your physical health and appearance, give yourself some slack on getting your finances in order and becoming a great cook. Whatever areas you want to improve, now that you dare to look at them, will wait for you to get to them.

6. Don't aim for perfection; aim for healthy progress. Give yourself permission to stumble along the way, to go three steps forward and two steps back. Allow yourself a degree of failure and a measure of grace from the outset.

PERSONAL EVALUATION

· Are you able to realize that admitting you have weaknesses does not have to mean you are a deficient human being?

· Since taking this journey, are you more willing to acknowledge your weaknesses and seek to cope with them in positive ways?

· What weaknesses do you not feel the need to change? Are there people you can relate to in a way that allows you to draw from their strengths and allows them to draw from your strengths?

· What are your strengths? How do you use them to help others who are not strong in these ways?

· What are weaknesses that you feel the need to change?

ACTION

List weaknesses that you can now acknowledge.

Number them in their order of priority—which ones you want to deal with first, second, third, and so on.

For the first weakness, use the knowledge you have learned during this journey to devise a plan to change your life for the better in this area.

REFLECTION

- How does it feel to be able to face yourself at a point of weakness and not conclude that you are forever stuck with yourself as you are?
- What positive changes do you think will occur when you have used the freedom from shame you have experienced as a basis for discovering a new way of life?

ENCOURAGEMENT

The courage and determination you have displayed throughout this journey will help you face and cope with your weaknesses that stand between you and the good life you desire.

FOOD FOR THOUGHT

If you accept your limitations you go beyond them.
—Brendan Francis

Finding a Counselor to Deal with the Roots of Shame

When shame is at the core of your self-image, there are good reasons to consider getting professional help from a counselor or therapist who specializes in dealing with the root issues of shame. Here are a few to consider:

1. Shame is often caused by emotional injury that occurred at an early age. The wounds and scars that originally triggered the shame might be invisible and therefore discounted as compared to the way you would treat a physical injury. If you were dealing with a broken bone instead of brokenness in the area of your emotions and self-image, you would not dare to try to treat the injury yourself. In the physical realm you realize that time alone does not heal. In fact, there is great danger in not getting treatment for broken bones because they can fuse together in a position that is out of alignment and cause problems throughout your body. The same is true of emotional injuries. You need someone skilled in identifying areas of brokenness, setting them in proper alignment, and giving you the life cast that will help you keep things in proper place until you have time to heal.

2. Emotional injuries related to shame cause a disowning of yourself at the core of your being. This tendency is characterized by denial. When

something traumatic occurred in your life that you interpreted to be caused by a flaw within yourself, you were shamed into secrecy, even within yourself. You can be cut off from all conscious memories of what happened so that you don't really know what you are struggling to deal with and resolve. A skilled therapist can help you experience the security you need to discover the truth of what happened that keeps you trapped in shame. Once you know what you are dealing with, the therapist can help you learn skills to resolve the issues, grieve your losses, and find a new way of life free from the hidden secrets that have hurt you.

3. A good counselor or therapist will be skilled at getting to the source of the problem instead of just dealing with the symptoms. You are probably more aware of the symptoms of the shame rather than the source; you focus your energies on dealing with these symptoms (physical, relational, spiritual, and emotional) that trouble your life. Let's say the source of your shame is like a faucet, the shame flowing through your life is like the water, and the presenting symptom or problem is like the end of the hose where the water comes out. Your life is getting flooded. On your own, you don't necessarily have access to the faucet. When you do your best to plug up the end of the hose, the pressure mounts in other areas, and problems or addictions spring up in the next place that can take the least amount of pressure. A good therapist can point out where the faucet is and help you turn off the flow of unhealthy shame at the source.

4. In a professional relationship with a counselor, you will find the clearly defined boundaries that provide a sense of security necessary for you to open up and reveal the truth you know about yourself. You will also be assured of having someone who will affirm, coach, and encourage you as you move toward a healthy new way of life.

Your shame may make it more difficult for you to admit that you could be helped by a counselor; you may interpret the admission of a need for help as admission that there is a deep flaw you are trying to hide. You can find the courage to move beyond this difficulty. You already have shown a desire for a new view of yourself and a new way of life by working through this 30-day journey. If you realize that your issues are not going to be resolved with a quick fix (and most people who are dealing with shame and are not in denial will realize this), be kind to yourself and seek professional help. Getting help can be a sign of health and hope rather than proof of your deficiency.

Perhaps you went to a counselor who was not able to help you or who used methods not in keeping with your values. Just because of that experience, don't discount all counselors. Keep looking until you find someone you can grow to trust, someone who has a reputation of helping others and shares your values.

PERSONAL EVALUATION

- Have you been able to identify and resolve the sources of shame in your life during this journey?
- Which of the reasons described here do you see as being valid reasons to seek professional help? Do any of them apply to you?
- Other than shame, what keeps you from seeking professional help?

ACTION

Make a list of valid reasons to seek counseling to deal with the roots of shame in your life.

Fold a sheet of paper down the middle. In the left margin, list the reasons you hesitate to seek help. On the line across from each reason, describe ways that would allow you to overcome the obstacle. You may want to ask your journey companion for ideas.

Do some research to find the name of someone with a good reputation for dealing successfully with issues related to yours. Call the treatment program the person is associated with or the office to get a consultation.

REFLECTION

Consider your hopes and reservations related to trying to find someone skilled at helping you. What would it be worth to you if someone really could help you get to the roots of your shame and deal with them at that level?

ENCOURAGEMENT

You have put in a notable amount of time and effort if you have come this far on your journey. If you need more help, I hope that you will demonstrate continued care for yourself by reaching out to a counselor. It is a sign of healthy shame that allows you to recognize your limits. If you have done the best you can and need more assistance, it is a sign of health that you can recognize that fact.

FOOD FOR THOUGHT

Where there is no counsel, the people fall;
But in the multitude of counselors there is safety.
—Proverbs 11:14

Evaluating Progress and Deciding Where You Go from Here

Although you have come to the end of the 30-day journey outlined in this book, your personal journey continues. I hope you now recognize that you can gain freedom from shame. Sure, you have unearthed areas of your life long buried that need continued attention, but every human life requires ongoing care. You are now in a better position to get help.

In the past, shame has kept you from going where you long to go, doing what you need to do to be happy and well, and reaching out for relationships with others, which you desperately need. As you begin to see ways to deal with shame in your life and you take the steps you can, you can gain freedom from the emotional terrorist called shame. Now that you have loosened some of the bonds of shame, you can ask for the help you need.

You have already taken decisive action to learn new things about how shame affects your life and have taken steps to gain freedom from shame in a particular area of your life. If you have experienced some degree of freedom from shame in that area, you can gain freedom in other areas where shame has a hold.

PERSONAL EVALUATION

On Day 7 you focused on reducing shame enough to move beyond some limitations imposed in one area. Review the sentences you completed on Day 7 related to how shame inhibited your life and what freedom from shame in this area would allow you to do. You selected one short-term goal to reach by the end of your 30-day journey.

- Were you able to reach your goal? If not, how far did you move in its direction?
- How has your self-understanding changed regarding this area? How has your life changed because of what you have learned and the choices you have made?
- What have you learned or considered that indicates issues in your life need attention and care?
- Have you found enough freedom from shame to be willing to reach out and seek help?
- Have you been able to develop a long-term plan for dealing with the roots of shame that influence your entire life?
- Look back through your journal and the personal evaluations you have made during your journey. What have you learned about yourself that gives you hope?

ACTION

Make a commitment to continue moving forward and making positive choices to overcome whatever obstacles may present themselves along the continuing road of life.

Sometimes problems are too difficult to handle alone on a 30-day journey. If you feel that you need additional help, please talk with one of the counselors at New Life Treatment Centers. The call is confidential and free.

1-800-277-LIFE